Mental Telepathy Affair Diary or Tides of Fate

Mental Telepathy Affair Diary or Tides of Fate

David C. Fitch

Ordering Information:

For orders and inquiries, please contact:
1-888-404-1388
www.goldtouchpress.com
book.orders@goldtouchpress.com

Printed in the United States of America

Table of Contents

Chapter One

Rick Annison managed an old town house on the east side of mid-Manhattan. The ground floor was used as a restaurant. The second floor was rented to a group of Psychics. The top three floors had two small apartments and thirteen single rooms, which were rented separately.

One of the apartments was rented to Mark Ingersol, a stock broker, who had moved there after his wife and he separated. At the time, Mark seemed to have a shyish half-grin when he spoke. He was about five feet nine inches tall, a little puffy in the face, had blue-gray eyes and his hair was thinning on top with a slight bald spot at the back of his head. He was neither wiry nor fat and seemed to open up to Rick in a talkative way, especially when he had a drink or so, which he handled well then. He lived there for a few months, in which time he went to see his twelve-year-old son living in New Jersey with Mark's wife's mother. During that time, Mark had little to do with women. Then along came Lauren Morgan—and when she came along, heads turned for more than a momentary glance. She was a stock broker. They met at an advanced seminar on stocks and bonds.

As far as Mark was concerned, it was love at first sight. Lauren had dark, black hair, smooth, white skin and was nicely formed with a Mona Lisa smile that had the feeling of a pleasant summer afternoon. The following day, Mark sent flowers to Lauren and invited her out for dinner. She accepted. She was separated from her husband who was considerably older and thought to be stingy with money, which Mark was not. She had no children.

Mark fell madly in love with Lauren, which he did not with his wife, at least not madly so. He could accept the separation from his wife and go on. With Lauren it would be different. His love for her was madness, in which you don't think rationally and about all you do is dwell on someone continually, constantly thinking of, and longing for reciprocation from that particular one, your mood depending on actions and reactions of one you are insanely in love with, and hopelessly can't feel the same about anybody else.

When Mark first introduced Lauren to Rick, the latter could see the chemistry between the two was very obvious there, in a big way. She was born in France of a French mother and German father, lived for a time on the French Reveira, and later came to America with her widowed father who was a doctor. She was cultured as well as attractive. She spoke five languages and there was a scent about her clan appearance that somehow reminded of a dozen fresh picked roses. On a scale from 1 to 10 she would have rated to less than highest. Six years younger than Mark, she looked closer to twenty-nine than her thirty nine years.

Lauren had a lease in her name on her large loft-like apartment, which she had locked her husband out of. About ten days after they met, Mark and Lauren found themselves so continually thinking of each other, they were sharing each other's thoughts—communicating with Lauren in her apartment by means of thought transference. He thought the apartment he was living in was hardly impressive enough for him to continue to invite Lauren into, which thought Lauren's mind picked up and passed thoughts of hers on to Mark, which his mind picked up. The two in their mind transference communication came up with idea it would be nice if they took up house-keeping together in her apartment, which is where Mark moved to.

After discovering they had a rare ability to communicate with each other by mental telepathy, they would find out they could communicate with each other by this means with great distances separating them. It has been said that a man and a woman who can do this have to be very, very much in love. Neither had ever met anyone else who could do this. Their mind transference with each other didn't seem to know the meaning of distance.

Mark and Lauren didn't mention to anyone their advanced mental telepathy ability, in which they could communicate in this means from at least as far as from New York City to various parts of Mexico—the furthest apart they would be later, fearing they would be thought of as "off base", bewitched, sorcerers, wizards or practices in witchcraft. They were secretive in this respect as far as others were concerned, feeling if others knew of this unusual ability of theirs, they would not only be questioning as to where this strain came from but wondering as to what other uncertain potentialities this couple harbored. Mark had read of thought transference between people but it was only of a nature where one person in a room would focus on looking at something in the room while another person in the next room would pick up what the other person was focusing on. For example, a chair or table, which paled in comparison to the thought transference ability of Mark and Lauren.

After Mark and Lauren took up living in her apartment, they went back to visit with Rick occasionally. The relationship between the couple seemed to be fabulous. After about six months, they saw Rick less and then not at all.

Then, when Mark and Lauren had lived together in her apartment for about a year, Mark came to see Rick, alone. Mark looked older, undernourished, broken-spirited and unhappy. He said he had lost his job and had a terrible argument with Lauren. He made Rick think of someone who had been shellshocked.

In Mark's diary is a subconscious stream of thought entry about the day of the terrible argument, depicting it in the heat of the time.

June 21, 1993   Diary to Lauren Morgan

Spent Friday afternoon with my ailing son, living with his grandmother. Worried about him. He will need a heart transplant. Feel hurt being out of work. Came home alone, ate, read and went off to sleep. Well, after midnight, Lauren came in after having been drinking. Said she only had three, didn't say how many times around. Possibly, going around in the back of her mind was something of me having lost my job and being around the apartment more. I was sober, having stopped drinking after I lost my job. She woke me up and a terrible argument got going. She was drinking and staying very late to spite me, possible revenge for me making but slight love to her for the past few months, due to my excessive use of alcohol which eliminated my sexual desire and performance through physical weakness, tiredness and nausea.

She and I continued the argument and she would charge at me, stand six inches from my face, hurl scurrilous, foul, vulgar and obscene remarks about my lack of sexual prowess and call me a homosexual (which I'm not) committing oral sodomy with all my drinking friends and bartenders. Her actual words amazed me. She started pushing me and I backed away, trying to persuade her to go to bed. She began to slap me in the face. I tried to block the blows. She removed one shoe, charged at me and began swinging at my face with the heel of her shoe. I tried to push her back while warding off the blows which might have struck my eyes.

In one of her charges, I moved both of my forearms, backhanded, to knock the shoe out of her hand and get her away from me and the bone of my right wrist accidentally caught her mouth and splintered one tooth as well as chipping another. At her request, I removed the remaining fragments with my fingers and found that both slid out.

Actually for the past years, her two front teeth have been loose due to a bout with pneumonia, which left one tooth longer than the other. In the year I've lived with her, she has undergone dental surgery a few times to even out these two front teeth, which surgery, while successful her teeth became even did not correct the problem of the looseness of the teeth. She had shown me several times how she could wiggle them back and forth with ease and to the time of this accident she had been undergoing surgery for several months to reinforce these teeth, which surgery had been unsuccessful. This was the case in each previous dental program for these two front teeth.

At the time of the accident, I believe if a cat's paw caught her in the mouth while jumping, her teeth would have been damaged.

After I removed the splintered and chipped fragments, I bathed her mouth and held Kleenex against her gums, which clotted quickly, I then put her to bed where she passed out.

She awoke around 6:30 a.m. and started drinking beer in the kitchen. I got up to talk to her and explain what had happened about four hours before. She was still high from alcohol and remembered little of what happened except that her two front teeth were missing.

I told her I was sorry about the accident and would take her to her own dental surgeon Monday morning to have her measured for a small front plate, for which I would pay the cost. She said OK. I kissed her, told her again I was sorry about the accident and went back to bed.

She waited until I fell asleep and, with more drinking provoking thoughts of revenge for what had happened to her teeth, called the police.

It must have been 9 or 10 o'clock Saturday morning when four police officers (3 men and 1 woman) marched into my bedroom, woke me up, made me get dressed, handcuffed me and drove me to the nearest precinct to be booked, while they sent her to the hospital where the police took the most unflattering pictures of her mouth with the teeth missing.

All my love to Lauren Morgan,
Mark

Chapter Two

After being discharged from a one-day stay in the hospital, Lauren had a court order drawn up prohibiting Mark from going near her.

How could he and she have become so unlike? The way they were about twelve months previously when she visited where Mark was living, Rick had never seen him happier than he was then. The two of them were crazy about each other. Mark wrote poems to and about her in the most endearing terms. Rick remembered one time when he knocked on Mark's door and Lauren was there and they were giggling like a couple of school kids. They invited Rick in for a drink and he sat there amused by their crazy-in-love antics.

"I feel a poetic spell coming on," Mark said.

"Silence everyone," Lauren uttered with a restrained shout.

Mark started with:
"It's nice to know the things you like,
A whimsy, caprice, a jog, a hike,
But what about the thought divine
That measures not with gold or wine,
A treasured love not always spoken,
In words and eyes and faith unbroken

> By a mundane world that moves about
> But never seems to sense the doubt
> Of things that are impermanent."

Lauren clapped her hands, adding, "Encore!"
Mark started with:

> "There's a moon out in space
> A cloud drifts over its face..."

"Continue," Lauren said.
"I'll have to work on it," Mark answered.
"May I tell you of young Father Malloy's second sermon?" she asked.
"Permission granted," he replied.
She went on with:
"Young Father Malloy was so very nervous at saying his first mass and sermon, he could hardly speak. After it was over, he asked his Monsignor for his comments. Monsignor told him he did fairly well, but suggested that the next Sunday he should put a little vodka or gin, instead of wine, in his chalice and by the time he got around to giving his sermon he should be a little more relaxed. The next Sunday Father Malloy was so anxious to do well he mixed wine, vodka and gin into his chalice. Being much more at ease, he talked up a storm. After the mass was over, he again asked Monsignor for his comments and they were as follows:

(1) There are 10 commandments—not 12.
(2) There are 12 disciples—not 10.
(3) David slew Goliath, he did not kick the shit out of him.
(4) We don't refer to Jesus Christ as, "The late J.C."
(5) Jacob wagered his donkey—he did not beat his ass.

(6) The Father, son & Holy Spirit are not referred to as Big Daddy Junior and the Spook.

(7) Jesus was consecrated, not constipated.

(8) And about your announcements of coming events: Next Sunday there will be a taffy-pulling contest at St. Peter's—not a peter pulling contest at St. Taffy's. Amen"

"I liked that," Mark said, and asked, "What did someone say to Disraeli? Someone said to Disraeli, "Lord Disraeli I believe you will either die on the gallows or from venereal disease." Disraeli replied, 'That depends on whether I embrace your principles or your mistress."

"They are not long the days of laughter, wine and roses, "Lauren swooned.

Mark turned to Rick with, "I find it impossible not to love her. Tonight I'll dream of kissing her a thousand times..."

"Have a pity on my poor lips," Lauren said.

"Each kiss more tender than the previous," Mark added.

"Her attractions cries out for lyrics

By more than we here have talent for..."

"I'll have to work on it."

"How many poems have you to work on?" Rick asked.

"I've lost count," Mark answered. "Nearly every time I look at her, a new poem starts forming:

'The moon tilts its axis

The better to be able to see Lauren..."

Another I'll have to work on."

"You should write a poem called "I'll have to work on it," Rick suggested.

Mark went on it:

"In a quite mood, listening to Mozart or Strauss

In a quiet mood, I find myself thinkin' of Lauren."

"You need a composer's name to rhyme with mine," Lauren suggested.

There was a knock at the door, it being Beth Scott saying, "I thought I heard Lauren's voice." She thought of Lauren as interesting. Lauren found her amusing. Beth, who was seventy-five, never married and getting along on Social Security and SSI, was one of those people who often seemed to have something humorous to come out with. "When a teacher asked a kid what memory is, the kid said, "Memory is something you forget with." Beth, whose wiry form of slightly over a hundred pounds extended to slightly under five-feet, lived on the top floor of the building, which didn't seem to deter her from walking up and down the stairs about as often as she pleased, sometimes so often she, as she put it, seemed to pass herself coming and going. She got along well with just about everybody. Someone around the place said that anybody that can't get along with Beth can't be gotten along with. She was a social drinker, sometimes more than that, pleasant, kind, considerate (when any one of the roomers was sick, she would try to help in some way, like a bowl of chicken and noodle soup) and generous.

She was asked by Mark, "Do you happen to know of a composer whose name rhymes with Lauren?"

"Classical or struggling?" Beth asked.

"Well," Mark added. "I guess I'll have...."

"We know," Lauren and Rick said in unison, "You'll have to work on it."

Chapter Three

Returning to what happened in their shocking argument which ended with Mark getting arrested and a court order being drawn up prohibiting him from going near Lauren, she, because he had no place to go, let him live temporarily in her apartment. They lived together about another week in which they had another big argument. It too, occurred on a Friday night.

June 28, 1993   Diary to Lauren Morgan

It was on a Friday again, exactly one week after the Friday we had the terrible argument, in which she alleged I knocked out her two front teeth, that she returned home around 11pm after having been drinking again. An argument ensued again about her drinking and coming home late for spite and revenge. I still love her but was much sicker than I realized and was unable to function sexually and, indeed in a lot of other ways, physically.

The argument was brief, vulgar, loud and obscene on both our parts. It lasted possibly five minutes and there was no physical activity of any kind. It was a repeat of many previous arguments, so I gave up and went to bed. This is what she refers to as harassment.

The following morning (Saturday), she got up about 9:00 o'clock and went to the bar across the street. I got up and watched her from our window. I had to leave the apartment for an hour or so, and when I came back I discovered a pin had been inserted in the door lock so that my key could not enter. I was locked out of my own apartment, shared with her, in which I had paid the full rent for all the time I lived there with her. The lease is in her name! I had no money, no ID card, Social Security card and everything I owned on the world, built up over a forty five year period, was locked up and access to any of it denied me. I had no money, nowhere to go and had only the clothes I was wearing.

I knocked on the door and called her name, to talk to her. I heard no answer, knocked and called her again. I waited and thought she might have gone out. I knocked a third time and called her again. As I was ready to leave, the police arrived. She had likely called them when I first knocked.

When they arrived, I explained my situation, actually my dilemma to them, and they were sympathetic—you can't be put out of your own apartment with no money and nothing but the clothes you are wearing. This would in fact make a street bum. As the police and I were discussing the situation, Lauren charged out of the apartment, obviously having been drinking, and launched into an almost incoherent tirade against me, using the most obscene, scurrilous and vulgar language imaginable.

She went on for several minutes, yelling, pointing her finger at me and speaking very rapidly like she had been taking amphetamines. She seemed unable to control her speech or pause for breath. Her eyes were wild with anger and hate.

I tried to remain calm and did on for several minutes. I then also became angry at her verbal abuse and what she was doing by denying me access to my own apartment shared with her for which I paid the rent.

I retaliated verbally and probably abusively as most people in the situation would. I saw the card later that day of me saying "I'll kill you," which was shown to me by a legal aid attorney that afternoon at my arraignment. I also noted that these comments were attested to by the arresting officers. In the first place, they did not sign this card in my presence. She must have prepared the card later, taking it to the precinct and had it signed. Unfortunately I was unable to prepare a similar card outlining her obscenities, since I was then in jail, and apparently, the arresting officers failed to record the obscene abuse she was subjecting me to. I didn't notice if the card was dated and the signature notarized. Even so, they may have been coerced or bribed to attest to these remarks which I don't remember at all. It is possible that under the circumstances and the heat and anger of the argument, I might have said something similar to what she alleges, but even so, these remarks are meaningless. How many times a day do you hear one person say to another, "I'll kill you?" I would not and could not hurt her in any physical way because I love her. My interpretation of the court order was that I was prohibited from harassing her at her work, in public places and in our apartment.

I didn't interpret the order to mean that I was denied access to my apartment shared with her where I was paying the rent and living there with her permission.

If there is a violation here, it is a tenuous and technical violation. The charges and allegations amount to a squabble and do not belong in a trial case.

When Lauren summoned police and said she was being harassed by me in spite of a court order she was misusing the term.

I was put in jail and sent to Rikers Island for twenty days experiencing brutal intimidation by police correction officers and inmates alike. It's a prison, where you are beaten, slapped, pushed, cursed at in the most obscene, loud and loathsome manner imaginable; where your clothes, toilet articles and anything of value are stolen; where you are pushed out of the chow line time and again for 'fun;' where food on your plate is taken at random according to the thief's taste and all deserts taken immediately; where you are slapped, pushed and tripped intentionally when passing an inmate or guard in a sullen mood; where you are made to give up your chair to someone bigger, or intimidated and threatened by two or three smaller creeps; where you are locked in your cell, sometimes for days without food, because a prison guard dislikes you for your color, intelligence or refusal to take silly, spiteful orders like scrubbing the bathroom and shower floors, sinks and toilets with your toothbrush; where you are constantly threatened with sodomy, sometimes tauntingly and sometimes for real.

These things you cannot defend or retaliate against because it makes it worse the next time. You are helpless to defend yourself in any way. You are frightened and fearful twenty four hours a day. Helpful sleep was impossible in the twenty days I spent at that Rikers Island Penn of hell, where torture in mind and soul becomes more unbearable each day.

That's what I call harassment.

Love,
Mark

Chapter Four

While Mark was incarcerated at Rikers Island, Rick received a phone call from Lauren. It wasn't the genial sounding voice he remembered being hers. She sounded almost distraught as she asked if he could find a room for Mark.

She made no mention as to why she and Mark would not be living together, probably assuming Mark had told Rick. It looked like, in her concern for Mark, she wanted to hear of him being settled in a room by himself. Rick told her he would see what he could do.

He didn't feel he should try to be an intermediary between the two since he had not been asked by either.

Chapter Five

After his twenty-day period of incarceration at Rikers Island, Mark came to see Rick again. He poured his sadness into Rick's sympathetic ear. "It was raining, very hard, the day I got free of Rikers Island. I borrowed a token from somebody and took a subway to mid-Manhattan. I slept in a cheap all-night movie house. Next day I went back to Rikers Island to get money and a watch which I thought I wouldn't get back. I returned to Manhattan and went to Blarney Stone bar where I hung around without drinking anything but ginger ale. I slept in another cheap all night movie house. Today, I contacted Lauren and asked her to pack some things of mine, a few clothes, shaving equipment and tooth brush in a small suitcase and leave it at the Blarney Stone, which she did and I picked it up."

Although Mark told Rick he contacted Lauren he did not say the means of the contact was by mental telepathy—this mind transference form of communication in which one can almost sense the other coming in, like expectation after one turns on a radio or television set. The sensed message can be clear, except when either is tired, at which times the sensed mind message can be faint.

Mark, having with him small suitcase told Rick before leaving the Blarney Stone bar he almost fell down from the need of sleep, finding his last two nights sleeping in all-night movies almost as restful as no sleep at all; and asked if Rick had a vacant room. All of the rooms were rented.

He asked if he could sleep in the large storage room on the top floor. This storage room had a large bath tub in it and a sink for washing, both for the use of the six roomers on the top floor. Mark said he would keep way over to one corner, out of the way of people who came in to wash and if anyone wanted to take a bath he would take a walk around the block a few times. He added he was paying four dollars to sleep at night in a cheap movie house and that he could pay Rick for the use of a small corner of the combined storage/bath room on the top floor.

Rick told him he would try to make it work and that he didn't want any of his money. But Rick did request Mark to take down to the street some items in the storage room that needed to be thrown out or given away to the Salvation Army. He also requested that Mark try to sleep there from after people on the top floor went to bed (11:00-11:30) to before they got up (6:00-6:30).

Mark cleared the storage room of items to be disposed of and generally tidied it up. Rick gave him a ground sheet, towel and blanket to soften the hard floor. In the morning Mark would pack these neatly in a designated place. Mark hoped he could go along with this arrangement until a rented room in the building became vacant. He also asked for a loan of thirty dollars, which Rick took care of.

Chapter Six

The storage room was hot in the late July weather. Mark was depressed and apprehensive, thinking of what others were thinking of him being there in the storage/bathroom from 11:30 pm to 6:30 am—although they didn't use the toilet there, that being further along the hall. Of the six roomers that live along that floor, not counting Mark, three were at the back of the building and three at the front. Mark, in the storage room, was in the middle. Beth was at the southwest corner at the back.

July 24, 1993   Diary to Lauren Morgan

Haven't made arrangements to start drawing unemployment insurance. Will contact former employee saying I've stopped drinking for good and will they please say I was laid off because of staff reduction rather than fired because of drinking. I miss Lauren and the babies (the two cats). My knees ache. My feet and ankles have swollen and hurt. Have to walk slow. Hope I can get enough sleep, even if the most I can get at night is about six or seven hours.

I'm very angry at Eric, at my former employer's, for asking Lauren to live with her at her place while I was at Rikers Island or not allowed at the apartment, and I'm angry with Lauren for considering it and not yelling at him and hanging up. There must be something wrong with her to even consider such a proposal. I would be embarrassed to mention it to anyone. I meant to tell her that Eric takes his pants down in the office when the boss is not there and also grabs his genitals in front of the men and even a couple of girls. If Lauren said yes to his request, he would surely take it as an open invitation to fuck her and would waste no time in trying to promote it.

I think of Lauren most of the day except when talking to Karl about Alcoholics Anonymous. He's starting to annoy me about going to meetings when I'm tired and don't feel up to being with a crowd of recovering alcoholics. I'll go again when I feel less unfit.

I won't contact Lauren unless it's necessary. Maybe I can see her Sunday afternoon. I still love her as much as ever and hate myself, but not as much as I did now that I've stopped drinking. I'm sorry for the pain, terror and grief I must have put her through, although I only remember part of what I did and even less about her feelings during this period, for me to understand the way she thinks and feels. This is, I think, in the most part, when she had been drinking, especially on Friday when she drinks heavier. She must know that almost all our arguments and fights came on Friday nights, the end of work week. Both times she had me arrested were for a Friday night fight. I very much want us to be together again as soon as possible and be happy forever. She must believe me when I tell her I'm having a very hard time now physically and mentally. I won't quit on my promise to myself never to drink again. I haven't seen any sign of her making a similar promise to herself. I don't want her to keep thinking about my past towards her when I was drunk, but try to remember some of the early good times. There were some times even in the past few months, when we were happy together, even if it was only a few hours, days or maybe a week or more.

I'll tell her to try to forget the bad things, watch my progress and look forward to a happy loving life between us in the future when time has eased and healed our anguish. It's hard for me not to be depressed, even when with bar friends, because I don't like talking to them and I don't like being alone. I only want to be with Lauren. I don't think I'll sleep well because of the apprehension about people maybe wanting to use this storage/ bath room for water when I'm trying to sleep. I love Lauren very much and will always. I hope after some time and distance between us, she will begin to think differently and lovingly about me. That thought alone can keep me going. She may not realize how extremely sensitive I am about things she thinks about me or says to me. Some things she says communicating in mental telepathy or in person made me angry and depressed. She must try to be calm and not unhappy. I love her so much and look forward to seeing her soon. Kiss for her and the two cats.

All my love to Lauren Morgan, Mark

Chapter Seven

In mind transference mode, Mark contacted Lauren—it being through the mind, his tiredness was discernible in the communication, the best time for each to get through to the other being is when the two were quiet and rested. Mark went over to some of the things he had written in his diary to her and asked if he could visit her at her apartment. She responded that she really shouldn't, in view of the alleged charges against him and the court order for him not to go near her.

July 25, 1993   Diary to Lauren Morgan

When Lauren seemed undecided on whether or not I could go to see her at her apartment, I reiterated to her some of what I had gone through at Rikers Island. She said she had heard of the place but did not know much about it and didn't really know where it is. I told her it's the world's largest penal colony where frightened officers say it's only a matter of time before the place explodes. The inmates now just about run that asylum. A few of feared inmates trade commodities like weapons, drugs, sex—a man and a woman. A quarter of the correction officers are women on that 415 acre island in the East River, accessible by a two-lane bridge, just off the shore-line of Astoria and only about 100 feet from a runway at LaGuardia. It's filled with murderers, rapists, armed robbers, drug dealers, arsonists and muggers. It's said 1 in 5 have AIDS. The inmates are detainees being held for trial or because they could not make bail. One of the inmates received through the mail a pair of leather boots and concealed in the soles were razor blades and marijuana. There're so many colored and Hispanics that control, that any time a white guy wants the barber shop, commissary, recreation, whatever, he's going to be the last. Prisoners today are younger, more vicious and don't listen to anybody. They make weapons out of anything— floor tiles, pieces of striping from the dropped ceiling. Some are ingenious at that, stuff up a toilet, making it overflow to create a diversion, then rob or attack someone. Gangs extort from other inmates, a lot of the young being strong, violent and uncontrollable. The jails have just become an extension of the streets.

I mentioned my present rundown condition with knees aching, ankles swollen and hurting and feeling depressed and in need of Lauren's company on this Sunday afternoon. She gave her OK to see her.

At Lauren's apartment, she told me her counselor had heard from the District Attorney's office that they may offer me a deal of three years' probation in lieu of me going to trial.

"It's excessive," I told Lauren, "for charges which are merely family squabbles, most of it lacking proof. It doesn't seem to be realized it's my first arrest at forty five years of age. Doesn't it mean anything that I've spent three horrifying weeks in that Rikers Island Penn, where I suffered two beatings by guards and inmates alike, theft of food and clothing, intimidation and threats? Most of the guards and inmates knew I didn't belong there on the charges alleged."

Lauren said she was sorry.

I asked her if she could have the charges against me dropped.

"So I'd be at your mercy again?" she said.

"I'm at yours," I told her. "At forty five I'm very old by prison standards where the average inmate is six inches taller and fifty to seventy five pounds heavier, more muscular and a street tough hard core in-and-outer since childhood. I'm not healthy and have suffered injuries from beatings. I have an inside nose split, infected ear damage and bruised ribs and back."

"I said I'm sorry," she said.

"I was hoping for something more. I think I've paid my debt to society by serving three weeks in that hell hole they call Rikers Island Penn and believe the charges should be dismissed on time served. At forty-five, I find three years' probation in lieu of going to trial is too excessive for first offense complaints and I'm too old to have a sword hanging over my head for that length of time. I could be dead before then."

"Ask your attorney to go after a better deal than three years' probation in lieu of going to trial," she suggested.

"Legal Aid Society attorneys don't have the clout of an attorney that gets a few hundred dollars an hour."

"I'll ask my attorney to go easy," she said.

"If they'll reduce probation to six months I might accept the deal—possibly even a year. If I go to trial pleading not guilty and am found that way, I wouldn't have to bother with any more of this legal nonsense. A lot of it can't be proven.

"A lot can."

"Like what?" I asked.

"Your verbal threats heard by police officers. You're breaking a court order not to come near me."

"Is it breaking a court order when you give your consent for me to see you? I suppose you could say you didn't give your consent—with your word against mine, and they likely will believe in you."

"Proof of breaking that court order to not come near me was established when you were arrested a second time at this apartment, when you weren't supposed to be here beyond the time I allowed you. Pleading ignorance to the authorities as to what a court order of restraint really means doesn't help you. As it is I'm taking a chance—you've told me you're going to kill me."

"Blowing off steam. You know I wouldn't harm a hair on your head, Lauren, and I've quit drinking now."

"I control my drinking, which you don't."

"When you came in after an evening of drinking in the middle of the night and woke me up and got into a tragic tussle with me, was that you in control?"

"You didn't have to knock my two front teeth out—you, who often said you were going to take care of me."

"I paid for all the rent here."

"In which you had full use of the place, including me."

"I haven't got the energy to go on. All I'd like is some sleep, peaceful sleep, in my old room for tonight."

She said, "OK."

"You won't call the police, saying you didn't give your OK for me spending the night here?"

"No."

I walked into my old room, struggled to get my clothes off, fell into bed and passed out.

Mark

Chapter Eight

Mark was up early in the morning (Monday), got something to eat for himself in Lauren's apartment, fed the cats and left. He went to the mid-Manhattan east Blarney Stone bar. Al, one of the customers there, said he could have a six-foot long white fabric bench with back if it was still in his old office. Mark thought he could get a dolly from the Blarney Stone to move it with help, and wheel it to his residence and have it lifted up to the storage/ bath room on the fifth floor. In the meantime he went to a discount brokerage office that was a competitor of the firm he had worked for and punched out some stock quotations on the computer.

July 26, 1993   Diary to Lauren Morgan

I feel if I had the money to trade, I could make money in the stock market now. When I was working and trading in stock options, I made $30,000 in a short time. Only trouble is I lost it all again trading in stock options. Next time I can make $30,000, I won't lose it. In working or watching the stock market's quick fortunes, computer-driven trades, the junk bonds, leveraged buyouts, options, you can get addicted to the glitz and glamour, danger and thrills. Some of the recent stock market upswings have looked as if they were going to last forever—with long bond interest, inflation, economic growth kept at median levels, on which the stock market seems to thrive. Aside from a sharp stock market correction in 1987 and a milder one in 1989, market corrections have been hardly more than what you could call digestions, in spite of the predictions of technical analysts, fundamentalists, astrologists and psychics among others. Some think when a stock is displaying sharp momentum on the upside it's time to climb aboard—going with the flow, the trend is your friend. But of course all of these have their other sides. For a while it seemed as if you could put up a page of stock quotations, throw darts at it, buy a group of those stocks with the dart holes and you could come out OK. Some think it's a good idea to stick to your favorites in the Dow-Jones average, some to emerging new stocks that'll hopefully be a new former IBM. And of course somewhere along the line these things are going to turn down, either in lightning strikes or in a manner of erosion a couple of points down, one up, two down. Run into are statistics which, according to the old way of keeping track of things, should have seen this market stalled and correcting more. It doesn't work the old way now, partly because people are plowing savings and retirement money into mutual funds, pension funds, insurance funds and trust departments of banks that used to go principally into bonds. And the managers of too many of these funds just throw it into the stock market. They want to keep their jobs, not wanting to be caught at the starting gate with a quickly rising market. And now it's the whole world investing in our market at an unsurpassed pace. In an interest driven market the Federal Reserve had learned to press the right buttons, including restriction and extension of money supply. We'll go into a phase where what'll matter most are profits when most of corporate downsizing is over. And there's the technological revolution we're in. New technical companies come out with initial public offerings that can go up 10, 40, 50% and more from their initial price in a day or so. Some think of today's as a gambler's paradise. In the 500-point market in one day in 1987, it looked like the floor specialists would have no option other than to fold. Some had run out of money and New York banks wouldn't lend them anymore because of lack of sufficient collateral, in some cases trading grinding to a halt. Then in quick time, the Federal Reserve Bank told New York banks they could let Wall Street, especially the specialists, have money they needed on loan immediately. But the investors and the little guys who had margin calls weren't given a similar life preserver. And if Wall Street specialists are not able to pay back all that was borrowed from the banks, which are backed by the Federal Reserve Bank, it'll be passed on so it filters down to the country's taxpayers paying for it.

When it comes to trading in stock options, which shouldn't be suggested to anyone who had not been around the trading scene for quite a while, I'll keep in mind that trading options places a premium not only on what I pay, but on time and good judgment about a particular stock. Paying much less for the option than for the underlying stock, I have the potential for making almost as much on one option contract as on 100 shares of the same stock—an opportunity to make a fat profit on a small investment. If I prefer diversification from one stock, there's the S&P index of 100 major stocks. For a stock I think will go down, I'll get put options. The seller of the option I buy will have an advantage over me, the premium involved working to his benefit.

After punching out stock quotes, I went to the storage room and rested in a chair. Beth came in to wash a pan. I told her I had stopped drinking and had been going to Al Anon meetings. She asked me if I'd like a cup of tea. Told her not to go to any bother. "No bother," she said as she filled a pan with water, put it on a small stove in her room and returned to the storage room. Told her about my Sunday meeting with Lauren. She was sympathetic. Beth's such a caring person. If you mention something that bothers, you she can mention something equally as troubling, if not more so, with her. She told me her mother lost her memory in an accident that left her with a piece of bone pressing on her brain. "My mother got to thinking I was a strange woman in the house," Beth said. "She said to my father about me, 'I have been married to you for over forty years and you bring a strange woman into the house.' And my father would say, 'That's just Beth.'"

I asked Beth what kind of an accident her mother was in.

"My brother had bought a motorcycle and he took my mother for a ride in it."

She was in the side car and they were going down a hill and something went wrong with the brake and he tried to stop with his shoe. They went down an incline into a wooden fence. My mother stood up in the side car. She would not have got hit if she had not stood up but she stood up and a piece of wood hit her so that her face was split open down the front, from her hair line to the bottom of the nose. Poor John. He was so proud of his motorcycle and to be able to take her for a ride in it. They were on their way back a different way and John asked someone the way and the person gave him a wrong direction. John felt so badly about the accident. My father sat up with my mother all night and she bled all night. Her face was terrible. It left a little scar down her face. She used to say when the weather got cool that it did something to the nerve there. It was over a period of months that she began to forget things, because of that accident. She was coming home on a train and she couldn't remember where she lived so a young woman on the train opened up her pocket book and found her address and brought her home. After that, we didn't let her go out by herself. Another time after that, she went out and went into a dairy and told the girl her name was Mrs. Scott and didn't know where she lived. My father went out looking for her and he said later when he was passing there, something caused him to look in and he found my mother and brought her home. My father was patient with her at the time. She was quiet. She would forget to eat if we didn't remind her and persuade her to. After that when I'd read or hear about a terrible accident it would bring me on a haunting feeling of my mother again. When I get into a craving for inner peace and quiet, I think of a garden I went to with my mother after her accident—a rose garden where we went for a walk. It was a lovely summer's day, just right, and we sat on a bench with the smell of flowers all around us. I felt happy and contented with the world. I get a yearning deep down inside me sometimes to sit in that beautiful garden again with my mother."

After tea with Beth, I found my feet and knees aching. Beth says at seventy-five when one part of her stops aching, another part takes over. I look with horror at the possibility of my ever reaching seventy-five. When you die young you're saved from growing old accumulating more aches, pains and sins. I slept so good in my old room in the apartment Sunday night. Am trying not to get depressed but it's hard with so many things up in the air. Feel uncomfortable and unsafe in this storage room with the door open. The fortune telling group on the second floor leave open the front door to this building from the street. Anybody can walk up past there to here.

There's a rumor Neil might be leaving. He's in the room next to Beth's at the back of the building—seems to be a middle-aged loner. If he leaves, I get his room. Tried to talk to him. All I got out of him were grunts. Beth says she'll try to talk to him to see if she can get more than that out of him. I figure I spend seventeen to eighteen hours a day now in the street or the Blarney Stone or sitting here after trying to sleep from 11:30 to 6:30 here with the light on and the door open.

No word from my previous office about possible job there. Feel forgotten. I'm almost absolutely lost. When I'm not thinking of myself, I think of Lauren. I feel the stress of physical, mental and emotional tension. At an Al Anon meeting, someone got up and said, while telling of her experience, if you want to shake hands with the grim reaper, stress can arrange a meeting real fast. Serious anxiety with the heart's contractions going wild can be a predictor of sudden cardiac death. A job can have a lot to do with stress, but not having a job can be as deadly. I told that to Beth and she said she had a bible in her room if I would like to borrow it. I told her I've read so many books on religion and philosophy I'm confused. Have got to stand on my own two feet. Beth said she would go to church and light a candle for me.

Saw Rick, the building manager. Asked if it would be OK to move the white bench with back to the storage/bath room. He said OK.

Love ya, Lauren.
Mark

Chapter Nine

It was Wednesday evening and Lauren had gone to the bar across the street from where she lived. The bar stretched from the building front well back to the rear where there were tables. Seated at one of the tables was a tall, middle-aged, somewhat handsome man eyeing Lauren, standing alone, drinking at the bar. How much importance is attached to the angle from which one person views another is arguable, but in this instance it was an angle that greatly favored Lauren. The man ordered a waiter to ask Lauren what she would like to drink and with her acceptance get it for her, with his compliments.

When the waiter asked Lauren what she would like to drink, compliments of the man pointed out by the waiter, seated at the table who had arranged this, she glanced over at him, hesitated and signified it would be OK. After vodka and water had been brought by the waiter, Lauren turned toward the man at the table who would be paying for it and shaped her lips with the words, "Thank you."

The man at the table moved his lean, 6'3 body to where Lauren was standing and said, "You're welcome." He added, "Would you prefer to sit down?" She nodded. He pointed to where he had been sitting, and as she moved ahead of him, he notice the way she swayed her hips.

"Care for something to eat?" he asked as they became seated.

"No thanks."

"I'm Sellner LeMay."

"Lauren Morgan, a stock broker."

"I'm into rapping."

"You're a rapper?"

"I handle rappers. I'm into it because it's the fastest growing and most notorious segment of the music industry."

"Reciting to music?"

"To a beat that turns people on. Has an audience of all races and incomes. Its style and stars influence popular culture."

"A couple of rappers were killed not long ago."

"Unfortunately, violence has not been absent from the picture."

How long has it been around—rap?" Lauren asked.

"It got going in the '70s with rhymes like:

> 'Throw your hands in the air,
> And wave them like you just don't care.'

Back then, people rapped for the fun of it. Then rappers got to getting checks and getting some ownership of a record company."

"Do you own a record company?"

"I made that a priority as soon as I could. I've always been interested in words spoken with stepped up beats touching on the culture of America and beyond."

"International too?"

"Worldwide—with a mixture of reality and fantasy, ferocity and meekness, poverty and excess. A world of huge successes and terrible casualties, put into rhymes about life's hardness, terror and violence, to meet a demand."

"To meet a demand?"

"With lyrics including,

'Beat up the police.'"

"That too?"

"Lyrics got deadlier as crack cocaine started laying waste to inner cities."

"You're also into drugs?" she asked.

"Drugs are a cash cow. I was only in for a while to get a foundation for what I wanted to do and because I knew what it was to be without money, like I know now what it is to be with it—lots of it."

"Which gives you balanced objectivity, I suppose."

"I make money because I understand the cynicism, perversity and lawlessness of drug dealing creeping into rappers' lyrics, reaching into the pained psyches of young Americans with lyrics including,

'F—k the police.'"

"To meet a demand?" she said again.

"Monster hits become so without radio airplay. Big money rolls in."

"Like in drugs?"

"Not that big. Drugs are too dangerous to stay in. It's not against the law to deal in rap. Rap isn't unlawful as long as the violence is only in the words."

"Words that have the effect of violence?"

"There might be a fine line somewhere, which the law is trying to figure out. Aside from that, plenty of whites find they can connect with rap with young adherents wearing pants with the crotch hanging down around their knees."

"Which I don't understand."

"Like another drink?" he asked her.

"Please do, while I tell you what I own besides a record company."

"Well, all right."

After ordering more drinks he told her he owned a television station, film company, management company, a magazine, a soul food restaurant, a clothing line, a building on Park Avenue, a home on Staten Island and a Cadillac.

"Can't leave you much time to handle your portfolio of stocks and bonds," Lauren said.

"I have a stock broker of course."

"I, being a stock broker wonder, if you're happy with him."

"Not as happy as I imagine I might be with you."

"Transferring stock and bond accounts goes on every day. I can get transfer forms to you if you wish."

"Good."

"Where will I have them sent?"

"Give them to me personally next time we meet."

"When will that be?"

"I'll phone you. Your number?"

She wrote it out for him.

"Like a drive home?"

It's near. I can walk," she answered.

"Take care".

"I will. Good night."

"Good night."

Chapter Ten

Mark hoped Neil would move as soon as possible. He was worried Neil wouldn't go and how long he could continue to stay in the storage room. He was tired and couldn't sleep well with the open door and noises in the hallway upsetting him. The only thing that cheered him a little was the thought of seeing Lauren and the cats on a Sunday, with her permission, and feeling safe, secure and comfortable for at least a day.

July 27, 1993   Diary to Lauren Morgan

Living this way eats into your brain and emotions. I live in terror with the thought my visit to Lauren may be cut off. Must contact her to let me know if the probation officer calls her and if he does, to let me know what she says to him so we don't get our stories crossed.

If I go to trial pleading not guilty and the judge says I'll have to serve 30 days in jail it would mean 30 days less 10 days off for good behavior less 20 days served at Rikers, making it equal to time already served. Do I go or not go to trial? I hate myself for what I've brought Lauren and myself to. I love and miss her more than she imagines. I took a pamphlet from Al

Anon with twelve questions, which you have to answer with yes or no. If you say yes to four or more questions, they say you are in trouble with alcohol. I answered yes to eleven. Then I took the test to Lauren (the way I thought she might answer) and she answered (in my estimation) yes to nine.

Went to see my son, living with his grandmother in New Jersey. A nice woman, almost over-protective toward the boy, and a lady—as her daughter, my wife, was once. We didn't think we could have children because my wife had a childhood disease, so we adopted a little girl, seven months old. We named her Ann Marie. Unfortunately, she was only with us a short time. It hurt terribly but it was partially offset by my wife discovering that she had become pregnant; and a son, David, was born—unfortunately with a defect that affected his heart.

Visiting my son, living with his grandmother, I was served tea, at which time the three of us enjoyed ourselves. The elderly lady was extremely fond of the boy and was doing an excellent job in bringing him up. He's well- mannered, handsome, considerate—the kind of son you dream of having—though not strong because of his heart condition. Though efforts are being made to get a heart donor for him, the demand is greater than the supply. Left visiting my son and his grandmother with a feeling of inadequacy—both fine people. Maybe someday I can do something much better for them.

Mark

Chapter Eleven

Why did Mark and his wife, who was over five years younger than he, separate? She was a graduate from a community college and soft-spoken as well as nicely formed—a polite lady who served tea in dainty little tea cups. She seemed to say the right thing at the right time. When she used to awaken Mark in the morning, it was in a gentle, loving manner, rather than pushing her feet against his back and shoving him out of bed as some wives do. She was most attentive to his needs. He couldn't believe his good fortune in having her, with the exception of her ailing heart. She got to need a heart transplant. A heart donor was made available for her. She went through a heart transplant operation.

Mark, when asked by an attorney, Hal Malady, whom he had met at the Blarney Stone bar, how his wife was coming along, replied, "In a strange way, after her heart transplant operation."

"How do you mean?" asked Mr. Malady.

"Come and see for yourself. You have my address. Come tomorrow evening," Mark answered.

The following evening, Mark's attorney went to Mark's apartment, which was in the Bronx at the time. When Mr. Malady rang the bell of the apartment, a woman about Mark's age, with a mug of beer in one hand, opened the door. Mr. Malady's first reaction was this was not Mark's wife, because Mark had said his wife was dainty and didn't drink. The woman in front of him wore army boots, blue denim pants and a lumberman's jacket. When Mr. Malady asked if Mark was in she said he had gone to the store to get something to eat. Mr. Malady said Mark had told him his wife had had a heart transplant. She said she was Mark's wife and that Mr. Malady could come in and wait for Mark.

Mr. Malady went into the living room where Mark's wife, Sandra, put her mug of beer on an end table, took out a cigar, lit it and asked Mr. Malady if he would like a cigar, which he politely refused. She then turned on the TV to a wrestling match and watched it with a cigar in one hand and a mug of beer in the other, while from a sitting position on the couch, she excitedly stomped her feet up and down.

"Excuse me," she said, "there's a chicken leg in the fridge my husband didn't feel like eating." She went to the fridge and returned with a chicken leg which she devoured, more in the manner of attacking it than eating it. "I'd offer you some if I had another," she said. After scraping all of the meat off the bone with her teeth she wiped her mouth on her sleeve, threw the chicken bone up in the air, caught it and took it to the kitchen where it was discarded. "I'm still hungry, goddamn it," she said while returning to the living room. "I could eat a cow. You look like you could too." Mr. Malady told her he was not a big eater. "Excuse me while I get another mug of beer," she said. "Would you like one?" When Mr. Malady politely refused she said, "Not a drinking man?'

"Only occasionally," he said. "Do you have a drinking limit?"

"I just keep on 'til I lose count," she said.

"How about your husband?"

"Oh, he drinks more time since I got my new heart, but I can drink him under the table," she said as she put her feet up on the low serving table. "What the hell's keepin' that guy? I asked him to bring something back for me. I hope he brings back a lot soon. Do you play poker?" Mr. Malady told her he wasn't much good at it. "I don't like playing cards with people I can beat easy. If that husband of mine doesn't come back with something to eat I'm going to get unladylike." She suggested Mr. Malady go looking for her husband, giving directions to the most likely places he had gone to.

Mr. Malady said he would do what he could and left. He went to where she had suggested her husband might be and, as he could not find Mark, returned to his residence.

Sometime later, when Mark met Hal Malady at the Blarney Stone bar, he apologized for not being at home the night Hal called at his apartment. Mark said he had bumped into an old acquaintance that evening and lost track of time. Mark also apologized for anything his wife might have said or done. "She's not the lady she used to be," Mark said. "I'm not the mild-mannered man I used to be. The chemistry that used to be very much there for us has gone out the window. From a soft spoken, dainty, mild-mannered tea drinking lady, she's turned into a beer-drinking, yapping, cigar-smoking tomboy. I'm getting to seeing her as more man than woman, and I'm not gay. Before her heart transplant, she couldn't stand the taste of beer and there was no way she would ever smoke a cigar. Now she can't get enough of them and she arm-wrestles with guys. I don't mean that develops into wrestling and sex. That's not the point. She's not unfaithful. If she keeps on the way she is though, I could be wishing she will be unfaithful so I can have reason to get away from her."

"It's that bad?" Hal Malady said.

"Some nights she'll use language an old sailor might use and she never used to even use the word 'damn'. And the way she eats now—I tell her, 'Slow down, you don't have to break any eating records. He added that the good care she used to take of her feet had ceased. "She used to have such lovely feet. I used to find it not the easiest thing in the world to get a girlfriend. I had wanted to meet a girl to admire her feet—like to regard with wonder and delight, to esteem highly. I love a nice girl's nice feet—feminine feet like Japanese girls have—the size and the way their soles look. I spent a lot of time looking for such a girl."

"Before you met your wife?" Hal Malady asked.

"Yes, I tried looking in magazines like 'Leg Show' for a woman who would like her feet admired as much as I liked admiring them. There were no women in my area with ads in those magazines."

"Isn't there a magazine called 'Foot Show'?"

"The nearest to it I know of is 'Leg Tease.' I wanted a woman who, not only wanted her feet admired, but was also interested in developing a friendship and more with me."

"How did you meet your wife?'

"The reason I had such a hard time before I met my wife was because of the way I came to women—like some droolin' creep. There isn't anything inherently creepy about being a foot fetishist unless we present it as so. Feet fetishism has a long, proud history, and some of the nicest guys around are into feet. But, with anything, there's a right and wrong way to go about it. By mentioning my obsession early and often was scaring women off."

"Was your wife a foot fetishist?"

"No, few women are, so if I had limited myself to women who shared my passion, I would have shrunk the pool of women I could draw potential partners from. I changed my strategy. I cultivated interests women would be interested in besides feet. A woman who may allow having her feet worshipped is likely not going to be interested in developing a friendship with somebody based solely on her feet. They want partners who have varied interests including sexually. I didn't go looking for a woman as into feet as I. I went after a woman who could show she was into me when I showed her I was into her before getting into foot fetishes. When I met my wife, I dated her without mentioning feet, took her to non-foot related movies and based our friendship on other than feet.

As she eventually agreed to let me kiss her lips, arms and neck I got down to kissing her feet. She asked me what I was doing. I said I was just admiring her nice feet. I didn't go into trying to do a lot of explaining. In further lovemaking, I always included her feet as though it was part of the package. I won't say she got to discovering she liked having her feet admired, but she did go along with me including it as part of our lovemaking. Now after her heart transplant, there's no urge on the part of either of us for lovemaking. Her idea of a real man now is not me and my idea of a dainty lady with irresistible feet is not her."

"Does Lauren have nice feet?"

"Oh yes."

"She didn't mind you becoming nicely acquainted with them?"

"She didn't mind".

Chapter Twelve

Beth, at Lauren's invitation, went to see her at her loft apartment, which had folding dividers rather than walls separating the kitchen and two bedrooms from the living room. It was sparsely furnished with quite well-worn furniture.

According to Beth, Lauren seemed to be having some kind of a battle with herself. She had not stopped drinking nor smoking and seemed to want someone who could take her away from herself. Beth tried, while joining her in a drink to get her to smile, telling of a maid's experience waiting on ladies at bridge party.

"Yes'm ah quit dat job. Dat were de mos' ridiculos place I' se eber been in!

Dey played a game called bridge, an' las' night dere was lots o' fellas an' gals dere. Jes' as ah was fixin' to serve 'freshmints ah heahs dis man say to a woman "Tak yo' hands off ma trick!'

Ah jes neah drapped daid when, bless may bones, ah heahs annuder man say, 'You sure got a nice bust!'

Den annuder man say, 'Lay down an' le' me see what you got!'

Den ah heahs dis woman say, 'You forced me an' ah had to take you out when ah'd already been down twice!'

Den dis udder woman say, 'You jumped me twice when yo didn't have stuff enuff fo' one good raise.'

An den some woman say somep'n 'bout 'coverin' her honor. Well, ah jist up and gits mah hat 'cause ah knowed dat ain't no fittin' place fo' me, an' jus' as ah was leavin', ah hope to die ef dis woman don't sya, "Well, ah guess we'll stop now, as dis is may las' rubber,' and' den—doggone ef she didn't say, 'Lay down yo dummy an' let me play on it!'

No ma'm ah's a lady an' ah jes' couldn't stay dere!"

Lauren smiled and seemed about to tell something and then changed her mind and said, "Sometimes I wonder if I, like Mark, am at war with myself and we're two people at war with ourselves at war with each other—maybe because being at war with each other takes away some of the at war with ourselves."

Beth, seeing Lauren was depressed, tried another tact, saying, "I worked at a hospital in Scotland before I came to America. I left the hospital to take care of my mother when she got into an accident in my brother's motorcycle. At the time I got going out with my fellow named Jock and, as has happened God knows how many times, I got pregnant. I told Jock about it when we drove in his car to a picturesque lookout. He said he thought I knew how to take care of myself. He suggested I have an abortion. I said I didn't want to. He said he wouldn't marry me if I didn't have an abortion. He had never said he would have married me any way at any time. While he was driving me back from the lookout and I was sitting in front with him, I felt like grabbing the steering wheel and running the car off the road and off what was like a high cliff. What caused me to hesitate was the thought the baby that was starting inside me would be killed!

"When my sister Jean found out I was pregnant, she said I couldn't come back into the house. We got into an awful fight and she knocked me up against the wall and my father hit her and I ran screaming up the stairs. She went to Ireland that very day. She never married. She was kind of a peculiar person. She had no patience. When my pregnancy was beginning to show she used to keep watching me like a hawk. She would watch my figure and I would tighten myself up. I would wear a tight girdle and tight bra so nobody would notice.

"I stayed in the house all the time. Sometimes I would go to bed with my girdle on. And I think that's what killed the baby. At the time I thought only of hiding my figure. The baby died of blood poisoning.

"The nurse told me the baby wasn't suffering. I was the one that was doing all the suffering. I was suffering the tortures of the damned mentally because the baby was lying there so helpless and they wouldn't let me pick it up. I never even picked it up one time. Not once. And that killed me. First, it was in an incubator. And then they moved it to another hospital because sick babies couldn't be in that hospital and it was outside in a little bed and they said I couldn't touch it. It lived three weeks. I wanted so badly to pick it up. I was afraid to say so. I had the horror that if I had more children they would die. I suffered so much pain when the baby came and then to lose it and everything.

Beth was crying when she finished and Lauren was joining in. "At least we're both having a good cry," Beth said.

Chapter Thirteen

Rick told Mark he had noticed he had the door closed and the light out in the storage/bath room at around 5:00 am. He requested Mark please, in consideration of the roomers on the top floor who use that tub and sink, leave the light on and the door open. He said one of the tenants asked if he was setting up an obstacle course for tenants to get in to wash.

Mark went to the Blarney Stone and met the man who was giving him the big white bench with back. He and Mark took a hand truck from the cellar and went to his old office to get the big white bench. They found it unwieldy getting in on the hand truck. Mark was left alone with it at the freight elevator. He managed to get it down and take it to the 40th Street and Park Avenue where it fell off the hand truck. A young guy helped Mark get it back on and they took it to where Mark lived. Mark told him he'd give him five dollars if he'd help him get it to the top floor. After the first flight of stairs, which nearly made Mark faint with exhaustion, the other man said he wanted ten dollars to go three more flights. Mark gave him all he had, seven dollars, and it took them another fifteen minutes to get it to and into the storage/bathroom.

July 28, 1993 am   Diary to Lauren Morgan

While lying in the storage room thinking of the good times Lauren and I have had, a short, bulky West Indian guy came running up the stairs from his front room on the floor below. He was swinging a large ax-like knife saying somebody had stolen twenty five dollars from his room when he left the door open to go to the bath room on his floor. He wondered if it had been done by somebody on my floor. I told him it wasn't me, adding I had no place to hide. He asked if I had noticed anybody come up to the top floor in the last five minutes. I said I had noticed Juan (a tall, 6'2", lean, young, Hispanic, who lives in the back of the building in the room on the north side) come up to his room.

"I suspect him," the West Indian said. "I need proof. I'll get it." He swung the knife he was carrying through the air and went down the stairs.

Feeling it would be nice to get out of the building a while, I went to an Al Anon meeting and had something to eat. When I got back to the storage room, Beth came in and said she had talked to Neil about a rumor he might possibly be leaving and he said he was planning on moving. I just can't believe that guy will ever do anything he says. Told Beth about the West Indian coming up the stairs wielding a big ax-like knife like someone in an old wild west war scene. Added I felt unsafe. She said she's used to feeling that way and that Rick gave her a whistle to blow if someone is seen up here that can't give a satisfactory answer when he's asked if he's looking for someone. Rick didn't give me a whistle, maybe 'cause I'm not a paying roomer. Sometimes I think I'm a nuisance around here. I asked Beth if she personally ran into any trouble up here.

"Once when I was in the bathroom here," she said, "someone came up early in the morning with a handkerchief covering the lower part of his face. He held a knife. He put his other arm around my mouth quick and hard and held the knife to my throat. I said, "Somebody is coming up the stairs. He looked to see while holding me and pulled me into the storage room. He put the knife up to my throat again and I was pulling down on his hand and that was when I got my hands cut with the knife and they were bleeding. Somebody who lived in one of the other rooms up here then yelled out of her room, 'What is going on?' The guy let me go and I screamed. I have a voice like an opera singer when it comes to terrified screaming. The girl who yelled out of her room came out and I was crying and she called the police. They came quick. I told them the guy with the knife to my throat tried to move up against the back of me. The policeman said, 'it's spring you know.' The guy with the knife tried to terrorize me. The girl who called the police said he was a sadist who enjoyed seeing me being scared. The next day, a detective took me down to see if I could identify a guy who had attacked a girl on the east side of the city. It was not the same guy who attacked me."

I asked when that happened. She said, "About five years ago." When I reiterated I didn't feel safe up here she said, "I'm lending you my whistle, cause I think you need it more than I do, in case somebody comes up that doesn't belong." She took the string it was tied to from around her neck and put it around my neck while telling me, "If I hear you using it I'll start screaming and we'll have the whole building aroused."

Lauren has no idea what I'm going through—all because of her two loose front teeth coming out in a stupid scuffle. But I love her.

Mark

Chapter Fourteen

Mark asked Rick if he thought the owner of the building would come around and ask about the big white bench being in the storage/bathroom. Rick said he didn't know. "If he does ask about it," Mark said, "will you please tell him it's only being used temporarily by someone that used to live in this building that's waiting for a vacancy to get in again, which is expected to be soon?" Rick said he would.

July 28, 1993 pm   Diary to Lauren Morgan

What if the owner doesn't like my having brought the big white bench into the storage/bathroom? What if he asks me to leave? If so, I don't know what I'll do. I'm becoming a terrible worrier. My knees ache bad. I might go to my former boss tomorrow and tell him I need a job and will work for no pay if he is short of money so that he can see that I'm sober and capable of staying that way (25 days now). Am apprehensive about sleeping in this storage/bathroom. Don't know what will happen in court but look forward to seeing Lauren and the two cats. Hot and humid in room. Looking out for intruders. An uncomfortable way to live. The people in the Blarney Stone (bartenders, waitresses and acquaintances at the bar) know of my situation and haven't been mean to me. Ask if I'm OK etc., although they can't help. June and July of this year have been the worst months of my life. The only positive thing that came out is that I got sober. I know that I'll never drink again and go through this kind of hell. Worrying me constantly is the suspense and apprehension about the future with me, Lauren and the cats together again in our apartment after getting work and patching up this mess I've made. I love Lauren and need her and need to feel wanted by her—being secure and happy with her. Dianne the waitress was very kind to me when she heard about my stay in prison. I didn't know that her husband is an Al Anon alcoholic, who doesn't ever mention to anyone. Every Al Anon meeting is different—some boring, some interesting, some depressing—a lot of people, very mixed up. When I hear them I'm thinking at least they have a place to live without the fear I have here. I almost always leave the meetings depressed, especially when these people who seem to know each other are joking and seem unconcerned about things. If I don't sleep tonight I'm afraid I'll fall asleep somewhere outside tomorrow. I'd like to go see my old boss tomorrow but I don't want to fall asleep while asking him if I can come back and work for nothing to get started again. I try not to let things bother me too much because I could get mentally distraught. I can't stop worrying about everything; but at least I know if I was in this position and still drinking, I'd end up back in the psychiatric ward. What keeps me going is the hope that Lauren and I can be together again and happy like we once were. I miss her presence near me.

While immersed in thought in the storage room, I became aware of a strange white guy hobbling up the stairs on a crutch. About 5 yards behind him 2 colored guys followed with black plastic bags. I asked the guy on the crutch if he was looking for someone. He said, as Beth came out of her room to the hallway, he wanted to use the toilet. Beth told him she was sorry but these were not public quarters and strangers were not allowed up here. "We don't mean any harm," the guy on the crutch said, continuing to come up the stairs. Beth came over to me, took the whistle around my neck and blew it, causing a piercing sound, like a police whistle. The reaction of the guy on the crutch was for him to run down the stairs carrying his crutch with him (he was no cripple), pushing the two colored guys ahead of him.

"Quick thinking," I told Beth. "I forgot I had the whistle around my neck."

"I didn't," she said, "because I put it there. You hang on to it. I'll get another from Rick. Like a cup of tea?"

"I should be asking you that," I said. "I owe you."

"Nothing is what you owe me. The tea won't take long." She went to her room to prepare it. Thank God for people like Beth.

Mark

Chapter Fifteen

Mark went to see his former boss. The latter was in the mail room using the copy machine. He told Mark he was busy and expenses were high. Mark let him know he was collecting unemployment insurance and had quit drinking and would work for nothing since he had seventeen to eighteen hours a day to get through while he wasn't trying to get sleep. Mark added he wasn't living with Lauren now. The boss was sympathetic and, although reluctant to let him come in and work for nothing, said he would think about it. He asked Mark if he was broke.

"Sort of," said Mark, "until I get my next unemployment check."

The boss offered him twenty dollars, which Mark went through weak motions of trying to refuse before accepting.

July 29, 1993   Diary to Lauren Morgan

While walking home after seeing my former boss, a taxi ran over a stone in the street which ricocheted to the calf of my left leg, causing me to fall to the ground wondering if I would ever get up. A tall, not bad looking, lean man about fifty-five helped me up and asked if I was OK. I found myself having to limp.

"Come on in here and rest a little," he said while helping me into a nearby bar. He seated me at a table and asked if I would like a drink.

"Thanks, ginger ale. I've stopped drinking the other stuff."

"I'll have the same," he told the waiter. He told me he was an attorney whose cousin was Oliver North's attorney. He added that he had been detoxed seventy-six times. Sharp guy—nice suit, hat and cane. Said he had just married a much younger woman and is already asking himself why. He assisted me out to the street, got a taxi for us and let me out at my residence. When he saw I was still limping he handed me his cane, saying, "Here, you need this more than I do."

When he drove off I hobbled up the stairs to the storage room and rested on the big white bench I had moved here. Creeping into my mind was the guy with a crutch and the two black guys following him up the stairs; and before that, the West Indian guy having money stolen by someone he suspects on this floor, and before, that some guy's attempt to rape Beth. Don't feel safe here—a lousy way to live. Thank God for Beth. She refers to this place as the house of horrors. Knees and feet ache. Hope Lauren does not forget to feed the cats after being out. Tired. Will try to sleep but doubt it. Too many noises in the hall. Love you Lauren. Miss you and the babies.

Mark

July 30, 1993   Diary to Lauren Morgan

Want to see former boss to start working for nothing but don't want him to see me limping with a cane. Will have to wait to see him again. Went to discount brokerage office, competitor of firm I worked for, and punched out some stock quotations on the computer with one hand while I sat on my other hand on the top of my cane. Feel if I had money to trade in stock options I could make quite a lot of profit. If I had the money the other day and had brought stock options in Intel, which I wanted to do, I would have done very well.

While making my way up the stairs, after limping back to my residence, Joel, a big homosexual who lives on the floor below my storage room said Juan was caught by the manager of the deli across the street hiding groceries in his jacket. When Juan went to the cashier to pay for a small chocolate bar, which he showed, the manager opened Juan's jacket and found tins of sardines, spam and beans there. I asked Joel if Juan had a regular job. Joel said Juan had worked for some messenger service as a messenger. He worked for about a year and got himself laid off so he could collect unemployment insurance for six months. Then, when his unemployment benefit runs out, he gets another messenger service job to work as long as it takes to get enough time so he can collect unemployment benefits again. He continues that cycle. Not the type you want to see your daughter marry.

In the storage room, Neil came in to wash his hands. Said nothing, so I don't know about his moving. Afraid if he sees me too anxious for his room he'll never leave. Tired.

July 31, 1993   Diary to Lauren Morgan

In mind transference mode, rising above the realm of everyday communication, I contacted Lauren. She let me know she stayed overnight in Westchester with a girlfriend. She made it known she would let me know later about coming to apartment on Sunday.

After Al Anon meeting, I felt depressed as I am a lot of times afterwards. Don't feel like going and hearing the same things over; but I know I can't drink.

Mark

Chapter Sixteen

With further regard as to why Mark and his wife separated; when Mark had talked to Hal Malady, the attorney, about his separation from his wife, he had been asked by Hal, "Have you wondered what the person was like who had had the heart that was donated for your wife?

"I assume it was a man," Mark said. "I would like to find out who it was. I doubt if the influence of a mild woman's heart could have had my wife acting as she has been. Of course, we were not in a position to be choosers—to find out if the personality of the heart of the donor was compatible with that of my wife. It had to be the first heart that could be made available. It was either her accepting it and living with whatever side-effects went with it, or dying because of no other heart donor being available."

"At what hospital did the heart transplant take place?"

"I'll get it for you."

"I'll see if I can get the name of the donor of the heart that went into your wife."

Chapter Seventeen

Mark phoned his former boss about working for nothing. The latter said he was sympathetic and would talk to the rest of the staff and get in touch with Mark. Following this, Mark went to an Al Anon meeting. Small turnout-ten to twelve people. When asked for a raise of hands for him/her to tell of a personal tale of woe, Mark raised his hand and told his tale of woe. To his surprise he was not at all nervous or ill at ease.

August 2, 1993   Diary to Lauren Morgan

After Al Anon meeting, went to see my son—such a nice boy I feel he's too good for me. No news of a heart donor for him.

Felt depressed as I returned to the storage room, where Neil came in drunk to use the sink. He said, "Hi." The only time he comes out with a sound other than a grunt is when he's drunk. Said he left the door to his room open so he could eye everything. Feel uncomfortable and unsafe. Wonder if Neil will ever move out. I hate this storage room. I love Lauren and apartment. Don't know what I'll do if Neil doesn't move.

Love you Lauren.   Mark

August 3, 1993   Diary to Lauren Morgan

No sleep. Too hot, too much noise. Beth gave me a cup of coffee in the morning. Went to Al Anon meeting where I listened to a lady's horror story. Meetings can be boring, but they say that everyone feels this way at times but it's important to keep attending. I figured on hearing some word from my former boss, but nothing. Managed to sleep in the afternoon from 4:30 to 5:00. Beth told me that Joel, the homosexual, had sixty dollars stolen from his room while he was in the bathroom on the floor below. He told Juan he suspects him. Juan's answer was, "You've got no proof". It's so hard to live this way. I long to get into a room of my own, where I can lock the door and turn on the darkness. Love you Lauren and the babies and the apartment.

Mark

August 4, 1993   Diary to Lauren Morgan

Went to Blarney Stone, where Rod Oakford came in with hangover from previous night and had a couple of vodkas before going to work.

No word from my former boss about working for nothing. After I got back to the storage room, a big fight broke out between Juan and Warren, a husky Jewish guy about six feet tall who lives in the northeast front room on this top floor. Warren had left the door of his room open while he took a bath in the bathroom where he had also left the bathroom door open a little so he could see what was going on. He noticed while he was taking a bath that Juan passed the bathroom going toward his (Warren's) room. When Warren got back to his room after his bath, he noticed $50 missing from a table there. Warren knocked on Juan's door to talk to him. There was no answer. Warren took a can of shaving cream and sprayed it on Juan's door to form A THIEF LIVES HERE. Juan opened his door, saw what was on it and asked, "What's that for?"

"You, for money that's disappeared from my room, like money that's disappeared from other rooms around here," Warren said.

"You have no proof."

"When I took my bath you were the only creep around. I left the door of the bathroom open a little. I saw you pass an' go toward my room."

Juan took out a knife. Warren said, "You want to play with knives. I've got one too. Juan dropped his knife, as did Warren. Then Juan called Warren, "a Jewish son of a bitch."

Warren went toward Juan in a boxing stance and landed hard lefts and rights. He had Juan groggy, backed up against a wall just about helpless. If Warren had kept hitting him he might have killed him. Perhaps sensing this, Warren ceased hitting him, leaving him to stagger groggily to his room.

Chapter Eighteen

As arranged by a phone call, Lauren met Sellner LeMay at Delmonicos for lunch. When they became seated and ordered drinks, LeMay, noticing Lauren with a large envelope asked, "What's that you have?"

"Stock transfer forms."

"Oh, yes, you would like to handle my stocks and bonds."

"How's the rapping?" Lauren asked.

"Do you know most successful rappers are colored? White rappers try to sound like them."

"Rapping is still gaining ground?"

"On rock and country and pop. Eating into me is the multi-million dollar underground market where bootlegged copies of tapes and discs are sold on the streets."

"You doing anything about it?"

"Law enforcement takes care of bootlegging. As it is, rappers are infiltrating mainstream television."

"Without some of the stuff toned down?"

"Not without some of the stuff toned down. Five of the R&B singles have been known to be by rappers. Rap is as diverse as people are.

'Hip hop is for real, I'm dealing with the truth;

All over the world is aggravated by youth.'"

"What is hip hop?" Lauren asked.

"An extension of the African-American culture. Like jazz, bebop and rock n' roll, it can be witnessed in music, language and fashion. Star basketball players sport hip hop inspired oversize shorts."

"Which I don't like—not nearly as sexy as the shorts as they used to wear. I hope pro football players never get to the stage of wearing oversize floppy pants in the game. I like what they wear now."

"Still, hip hop and its baggy oversize fashions have been the biggest influence on men's fashions in recent years in apparel and fragrances."

"Fragrances? How can you tell if a fragrance is rap inspired?"

"Ask an ad agency. They capitalize on the flood of money hip hop is generating. We have commercials with rap music. Cinemas are with commercial films with rap soundtracks. I might as well share with you that I'm as good as separated from my wife. She lives in one section of our large house and I in another. Both our kids, a boy and a girl, are in college."

"After being separated from my husband, I got into an affair with a stock broker who seems to have messed things up."

"You're still living with him?" Sellner asked.

"He comes to visit occasionally."

"Letting him down easy?"

"Something like that."

"Like another drink?"

"I have another appointment."

"I'll call you."

Chapter Nineteen

Mark phoned his former boss again about working for nothing, reiterating his arguments for needing the work. The boss couldn't seem to make up his mind. He finally said to Mark he would call him Friday; otherwise, to come in Monday, but no pay.

August 5, 1993   Diary to Lauren Morgan

In the afternoon, went to see my son, living with his grandmother in New Jersey. Broke my heart to go there. A fine well-behaved kid. They're still looking for a heart donor for him. Coming back from there, I got to thinking:

> Through want of a nut a bolt was lost,
> Through want of a bolt a tread was lost,
> Through want of a tread a tank was lost,
> Through want of a tank a battle was lost,
> Through want of a battle an empire was lost.
> So through want of a nut an empire was lost.

And through want of Lauren's two front teeth I'm lost.

Felt depressed when I got back to my storage/bathroom. Beth probably sensed it when she came in to wash her hands because she asked me if I'd like a cup of tea. I followed her to the table in her room by the open door and sat down. I told her I might be going back to doing some work at my old job for no pay to get my foot in the door again. She said she had a job with the Johnson family once, the best she ever had and then lost it through no fault of her own. "Mr. Johnson," Beth said, "was a big executive with the Johnson drug company. He was divorced and had married a physically beautiful model, one of those people who is so in love with her body she's afraid to bear children for fear her body will lose some of its shape. I took care of Mr. Johnson's daughter, Shiela, who was three and the step daughter of his current wife. While with them six months, I went to Nassau with them for about three months. They had a house there and the help went down. I loved it there. I was very happy there. I didn't work hard. I just took care of Shiela and she wasn't hard to handle. I loved her very much and she adored me. She used to call me her sweet little nursey nursey and I would call her my sweet little Shiela Shiela. The water there was nice and warm and the beach was cool coral. It was a private beach. While there, I had two operations on my eyes. Three quarters of the tear glands were taken out because my eyes were running water all the time. Mr. Johnson paid for the operations. When I was back from the hospital about a week, Shiela told her stepmother, 'I don't like you.' Sheila showed she was very fond of me and the step mother was jealous of it. The step mother hardly ever saw the girl. She saw the girl about a half an hour before Mr. Johnson came home and played with her and put on a big act. The child was starved for love and affection when I went there and I gave it to her. She was a miserable little girl and I changed all that. Mr. Johnson was grateful to me. As soon as I saw the look across the step mother's face when Shiela told her she didn't like, her I thought, 'Oh, oh, this doesn't look good for me.' I said, 'Shiela didn't mean that.' Next day the step mother said she was going to get a governess for Shiela to teach her French, meaning she wouldn't need me. I was heart-broken because I was so fond of Shiela. I cried and I cried. The step mother took Shiela away the whole day when I packed and left. I didn't get a chance to say goodbye to Shiela. The step mother liked young men and liked to be flattered and would make Mr. Johnson jealous. She was very beautiful. Having said that I'll say she tried to get the chauffeur fired but Mr. Johnson wouldn't fire him. She did fire the other help though. She was like a greedy child. She took everything and gave nothing. She was well-heeled with jewelry. She was a model before he married her. She was chosen out of eight hundred women to model for Jean Pateau, a French designer. She was very spoiled. She liked Nassau because she was made a big fuss of down there, but in Princeton they liked Mr. Johnson's first wife and didn't make much of a model, which was Mr. Johnson's second wife. I hear later Mr. Johnson divorced the model too. The places I could have gone with the Johnson family but for that second wife. She didn't like people who didn't make a fuss of her. I thought to myself, someday, lady, you're going to be out on your ear; and I hope to live to see that day, and I did. Mr. Johnson was crazy about Shiela. If I even bought Shiela a lolly pop, I get the money back. Sheila and I had the best state room on the ship. Mr. Johnson did his business from down there by phone. He had a yacht. When there are words between a nurse like me and the wife you know who goes. That second wife of his did me out of a lot of nice things that could have been done for me. It was the nicest job I ever had and she just squashed it. And I loved Shiela because she needed me so much. That was a mean thing that stepmother did. When I first went there, Shiela was so sad looking. Her hair was straight and I curled it. And we'd go out on a raining day and she would splash in all the puddles she wanted to because she had never done any of those things. She just blossomed with it all. I'll never forget the first time I saw her in that big nursery all by herself with toys she didn't play with. We would play house and have tea parties. She had little granaphone records and I sang with her and read to her. The step mother just married Mr. Johnson for his money and position. She was like a show piece for him. He wanted children but she didn't, being afraid it would get her body out of measurement. She was always getting herself measured and looked good in shorts. She had a stunning figure. There was no getting away from it. She was blond with big blue eyes. She had her own room and he has his own room. She was so jealous of Shiela because her father was crazy about her and Shiela was crazy about him. Shiela was adopted by him when she was a child but I think he was the father because she walked exactly liked him. I saw him walking along the beach and it came to me in a flash how Shiela had that certain same way he had. Shiela was dark complexioned with dark eyes, Latin type and a little tempermental. Mr. Johnson's first wife was not Shiela's mother. Mr. Johnson set his second wife's brother up in a practice as a dentist. Mr. Johnson wasn't happy with her. She was just out for all she could get. He had had everything handed to him on a silver platter and when it came to choosing women, he chose that wrong one. He paid his help well. He played tennis and went horseback riding. His clothes were always spotless and immaculate. You could see your face in his shoes. His room had everything in its place. The woman he was then married to had nothing to do but look beautiful. What a wardrobe she had. She used to get things made for her. And what gorgeous jewelry she had. If diamonds are a girl's best friends she had plenty of friends."

"I never got very close to someone that wealthy," I told Beth.

She said they have problems like you and me but in an expensive setting. While she was telling of her experience with the Johnson family with a soulful tone in her voice and a half conscious memory state, it had soothing effect on my state of mind.

With aching feet and knees I returned to the storage room.

Love Lauren and the apartment. Hope I can get up there over the weekend.

Mark

Chapter Twenty

Further regarding why Mark and his wife separated. Hal Malady, after acquiring the name of the hospital where Mark's wife had had her heart transplant, was able to get the name of the heart donor that went into Mark's wife—it being Jared Lyles of Staton Island, New York.

Mark and Hal Malady went to Staten Island and met with Mr. Lyles about the heart donor that went into Mark's wife. Mr. Lyles said the heart came from his son, Jared Jr., who was killed in a motorcycle accident.

"What kind of a man was he?" Mr. Malady asked.

"Jared Jr. was about five feet eleven inches, husky and spent some time in the navy. After that he worked in construction and did some amateur boxing—winning fourteen fights and losing three."

"Did he smoke or drink?" Mark asked.

"Some cigars and drank beer, except when he was training for boxing. He would sit in front of the television set with a glass of beer in one hand and a cigar in the other hand and watch boxing matches."

"Did he do much fighting out of the ring, or arguing?" Hal asked.

"He could hold his own in most fights or arguments. He got involved in a motorcycle gang. They would travel, almost a dozen of them, on their motorcycles around the countryside into the night. They went to Las Vegas as well as Atlantic City. Was on one of those motorcycle trips that his motorcycle got out of control and ran into a huge trailer. He was killed instantly."

"How old was he?"

"Twenty-seven. Never married."

After leaving Jared Lyles, for which he was thanked for his information, Hal Malady said to Mark, "You try to find answers and sometimes what you run into are questions that need to be answered. Cold Jared Lyles Jr. be blamed for your wife's actions? Could she have inherited with his donor heart his temperament?"

Chapter Twenty One

August 6, 1993   Diary to Lauren Morgan

Lauren contacted me, in a mind transference mode, making it known my unemployment check, sent to me at the address of her apartment, was there. Asked if I could come over. She said OK, adding that the communication she was receiving from me was not too clear—it being through the mind, the clearness of the communication depending on how non-tired, relaxed and fresh the mind is. She could tell in that way I was feeling low.

Arrived at the apartment around 4:00 p.m. Lauren had been drinking—talked silly, affectionate, repetitive all evening. Threatening for attention and affection ("If you don't want to talk to me then leave.") the apartment looked sloppy—ashes on tables, dishes not put away. Cat litter dirty. Ate at 7:00 p.m. and after that she left leftovers and dishes on the table and went to sleep for four hours. She sleeps and watches TV. I'm very tired. Don't know why I want her any more although I love her and the apartment and the cats. She doesn't seem to cope or see everyday reality as it is. Seems unable to plan ahead. She lets things slide. Doesn't appear to know if she wants me at the apartment or not.

Mark

August 7, 1993   Diary to Lauren Morgan

Today seems like a repeat of the latter part of yesterday in the apartment. When Lauren has been drinking, so she hallucinates does she identify her teeth being knocked out as something done on purpose by me? Does she suspect me of downplaying the incident as much as I suspect her of overplaying it? If only we could have the page of that day torn out of the book of our lives.

I asked her not to get connected with some undesirable that might have AIDS because my plans are for us to get back together again for good after I get to working and earning money again. I asked her again if the court order against me could please be lifted. She said we had gone through this before and it would be best left as is. Whatever love she has seems to amount to allowing me some weekend time with her, in which permission has to be obtained first. And then, there's the question of how long even this will last.

Mark

August 8, 1993   Diary to Lauren Morgan

Lauren appeared less high today. Around 10:30 a.m. she complained of heart palpitations, shortage of breath, tingling in hands and feet, difficulty in swallowing. Gave her an aspirin tablet. Before this, she thought she needed to go to the hospital. I feel uncomfortable being in the apartment with her, especially after that episode.

She scares me. I don't know what thoughts she may have in her mind. Is she afraid of me? Does she want to threaten or punish me more? I never know what she might do when drinking—especially when she's out by herself and drinks. She may have scotch or vodka hidden in the apartment. The situation has me off balance. She makes me mad unintentionally and with implied threats.

I don't know what will happen about Neil's room, the job, etc. I just know whatever happens, I must stay sober.

Mark

August 9, 1993   Diary to Lauren Morgan

Left apartment early. As I found myself able to walk without limping, I went to the stock brokerage firm I had worked for to see my former boss. He told me he told the staff that I'll just be helping out, that I'm not part of the staff and I take or make no business calls. Worked from 9:30 to 12:00. At noon, I went into the discount broker office of one of our competitors and punched out some stock quotations on the computer. A guy there said to me, "I haven't seen you for a while." I said to him, "I didn't think you remembered me." He said, "I'll remember you as long as I live. I'll tell you why. Last time, I saw you in here you had a cane…" I said, "I had hurt my leg and needed a cane then." He said, "Well let me tell you. While you were getting stock quotes then, you used the cane as a stool, resting one hand on the handle of the cane and sitting on that hand. It struck me as something out of Charlie Chaplin. I'll never forget it." It's funny what people remember you for. Would like to get back into trading in stock options when I can get funds together for it? If I could get a few lucky runs in stock options I could be on my way again. After work, went to two Al Anon meetings. Am still inhibited in speaking. Back to storage/bath room, I waited 'til someone in there finished washing up. Can't wait to get some privacy. I know if I was drinking through all this, I would never survive.

While resting in the storage room Juan came in and asked me if I could change five dollars. I took seven one-dollar bills out of my pocket and give him five for a five dollar bill from him. After I returned my seven dollars to a rear pocket in my pants, Juan went back to his room. I lay down on the bench to rest and dozed off to sleep. When I woke up I went to the deli across the street for a soft drink and when I went to pay for it I noticed the money I had had in my back pocket was gone. I thought of Juan. He had noticed which pocket I put my money in after I changed his five-dollar bill. He probably asked me to change it so he could find out which pocket I took from and returned my money to. When I had dozed off he must have sneaked in the storage room and slid the money out of my pocket. Here I am trying to get money together to buy stock options and that monster is stealing from me.

August 10, 1993   Diary to Lauren Morgan

Worked 'til 10:00 a.m. and went to nearby Citibank branch to open savings account. Can't hold any large amount of money in an open room with Juan around.

Can't help feeling everything is going against me—Lauren having the apartment, my former boss, the Court system, Neil not moving, that monster Juan, sleeping in a storage room when I should be in the apartment where Lauren is, being on my feet so many hours a day with my knees killing me. How I didn't protect myself:

1. Never saved my money.
2. Never kept old room (I left to go live with Lauren) for emergency.
3. Never got lease in my name on the apartment.
4. When I paid the rent on the apartment it was with money order without my signature.
5. Didn't protect my job.

6. Didn't take care of my health.
7. Put myself at the mercy of Lauren and the Court system.

Am getting angry at the whole hopeless scene. I question whether Lauren can handle herself. Tries to protect herself at my expense and seems not unhappy over position she has me in. She said when I communicated with her last night that the Strang Clinic doctor said she may be suffering from anxiety. Sounds possible from the way she acted the last weekend I was with her. Don't think she can handle money, the apartment, job, drinking and smoking, relatives and counselors giving her advice. I worry about her, the cats and the apartment, but don't know what to do about it as she is completely changeable in manner from day to day.

It's now 11:00 p.m. here in the storage/bathroom and Neil is at the sink, where has been for the past fifteen minutes, brushing his teeth, drunk and naked. He said he may move sooner than I think. Then he says, "Mark, could we go some place for a few minutes?"—a drunk proposition. How much more do I have to endure?

Chapter Twenty Two

Mark worked until 3:30 pm and went to an Al Anon meeting, finding it half depressing—but it killed time, he thought, and provided misery for misery.

August 11, 1993   Diary to Lauren Morgan

Beth said Neil told her he is moving this week. I saw Neil later and he said nothing. I hate living here after being in the apartment. I feel cheated with no convenience, no privacy, no Lauren and no cats. Completely unfair and I can't seem to do anything about it at present. Can't rush Lauren because she's too mixed up to make up her mind.

I think if I stick it out with my boss and work hard everyday, something positive will come out of it. Must stay sober.

Love you, Lauren.
Mark

August 13, 1993   Diary to Lauren Morgan

Had coffee with Beth and went to work early. At lunchtime, went to Al Anon meeting. Heard a very powerful speaker who was a Catholic school teacher for ten years. Very forceful, sometimes funny, went back to work where at 4:30, the boss gave me $75 cash. Told him I didn't expect it (although I was hoping) and appreciated it even if it's only about $15 a day or $2 an hour with no health or other kinds of benefits. Worked until 4:45. After leaving office, my knees and back ached, so I had to rest on the way to meet Lauren at the corner of Madison and 38th Street.

I told Lauren I felt old with loss of weight, aches and almost no strength in my arms. This and not getting any sleep, very little rest and being on my feet so much is too much for me. Lauren told me a doctor said she has no lung or heart symptoms and feels her problem is anxiety. She took me to her apartment. I felt so good and comfortable there compared with the storage/bathroom I'm trying to get out of.

Lauren still making no decision about me coming back. I doubt if she thinks about anything at all except her own problems. I have to go to court on August 31st, at which time the three-year probation may become effective. I want to go back to the apartment but not with a three-year court order prohibiting me from going there. Also, if I go back, I want my name to be on the lease(which might cause another war with her). She is so unstable I feel very uncomfortable in trusting her with anything. What would she do if she gets an attack of anxiety or whatever if I'm not there? If I am there, I would hesitate to call an ambulance in case they send the police with it. What happens to the cats if she is hospitalized? Supposing she is in a coma and/or can't speak. I'm very upset, especially since she does not even understand how serious it is for both of us. She must think about all this now as Court date is August 31st and rent renewal is in September, I think. She must reach some decision on her own without listening to others who do not know the facts.

Around 9:00 p.m., the phone rang. As Lauren was taking a shower, I answered it. A guy asked for Lauren. I asked who was calling. He said, "Sellner LeMay." I told Lauren who was on the phone for her. She stepped out of the shower, threw a robe around her, went to the phone and talked for about ten minutes, in hushed tones.

Mark

Chapter Twenty Three

Mark, on a visit to his son, living with the boy's grandmother, told this woman, his mother-in-law, he had found out who the owner was of the heart that had gone into his wife—it being Jared Lyles, Jr. Mark passed on to her that Jared Lyles, Jr. was killed in a motorcycle accident. He had spent time in the navy, done construction work and some amateur boxing. When not training, he smoked cigars and drank beer. He had belonged to a motorcycle gang.

Mark's mother-in-law asked if Mark had talked to the surgeon who performed Sandra's change of heart operation. Mark said he had, and the surgeon said he thought her taking on a different personality could partly be explained as an identity crises brought on by trauma of surgery.

"This surgeon recognized characteristics of the previous heart owner passed on with his heart to Sandra?" Mark's mother in law questioned.

"He recognized that, along with the trauma of surgery."

Mark's mother-in-law wondered if Sandra could be taught to be her former sweet, gentle, subdued self at a finishing school for women.

Chapter Twenty Four

Mark was worried at the office thinking of Lauren talking to Sellner Lemay in hushed tones on the phone. It seemed she had given another guy her phone number.

August 16, 1993   Diary to Lauren Morgan

During lunch period, I went to nearby discount stock broker and punched out stock quotations on the computer. The guy who said I reminded him of the Charlie Chaplin was there going through the Wall Street Journal in which he was making all kinds of pencil marks besides stocks selling under five dollars.

After work, went to two Al Anon meetings. I felt uncomfortable as I was unsure about speaking and didn't. Felt like leaving after first meeting but more people came and I didn't want to go back to storage room so stayed for second meeting.

Back to storage room, where I saw a tall wiry Norwegian guy called Erik, who lives two floors below, come up the stairs with another big guy, who seemed to be Norwegian. Erik asked me where Juan lives. I told him. He knocked on Juan's door. When Juan opened his door, Erik and his friend started pounding on Juan's face and body with their fists as hard as they could, knocking him out. Juan lay there with two black eyes, swollen cheeks and a bloody nose and mouth—a mess. Erik then went into the bath room, ran water into a pail, took it into Juan's room and dumped the water over Juan. As Juan started to regain consciousness, Erik said, "That's for tryin' to make out with Elise." He and his friend then went down the stairs.

Chapter Twenty Five

When Rick heard of Erik, the Norwegian fellow who lived on the third floor, and a friend knocking Juan out, he contacted Erik about it.

Erik said his girlfriend, Elise, hopeful of becoming a big time model, who was visiting him, went across the street alone to get a bottle of wine and while returning through the lobby of the building, a tall fellow, who had over his head a paper bag with two small holes which his eyes saw through, approached her with a knife, lifted up the front of her dress and tried to rape her while standing up. When Elise, in struggling, tore the bag on the guy's head, revealing Juan, he ran out the front door of the building and disappeared. Elise went to Erik's room and told him of what had happened. She said it was Juan that did it. Erik said he then called his friend and the two of them visited Juan to take care of him. Erik also said Elise was going to contact the District Attorney's office to place a charge of attempted rape against Juan.

Juan was put in jail. The bail amount was $500, which his mother came up with to get him out. She worked for New York City as a subway train operator. When anything happened to Juan in connection with the law, he called his mother who would proceed to counter any allegations against her son before she knew the facts. If she brought him up that way, it could have been partly what was wrong—refusing to believe her son did anything wrong, rather than correcting him when correction was called for.

She went after a legal aid society attorney for Juan, saying as her son had often said, "There's no proof."

Rick said that if the matter went to trial and Juan is found guilty he would go for a part of the sentence being that Juan must leave this building; or if a deal is made, part of the deal be that Juan must leave the building with a court order restraining him from coming back to the place.

Chapter Twenty Six

Mark was told by Beth that she had not seen Neil yesterday, nor the day before. It was noticed there were two locks on Neil's door. "If he's trying to make his leaving look mysterious, he's succeeding," Beth added.

August 17, 1993   Diary to Lauren Morgan

At office, little work to do. At lunchtime, punched out stock quotations at a nearby discount stock broker's. Am hopeful I can get enough money together to get into buying stock options, which could be a possible way out.

Went to AA meeting after, which was very crowded. There, a member, who used to be a bad drunk that was barred from Billy Buds several times, gave me a book called "Living Sober".

Went to storage bathroom and tried to collect my thoughts. Am mad over living this way and incensed at Lauren's appearance of indifference about my situation. I want to get back to the apartment as soon as possible. Have been very lonely since not living there on a full-time basis and feel that nobody, with the exception of Beth, my son and his grandmother, cares about me. Lauren doesn't know how hard it is for me mentally, physically and especially emotionally.

Must stay sober. Since I might not be getting back on payroll before unemployment insurance expires I'm thinking of applying for Social Security Disability. This could take some time. I should start working on it now. Saw an attorney that comes into the Blarney Stone bar and talked to him about it. He asked me what claim I had in mind. I said substance abuse.

Attorney: Like what?
Me: Alcohol dependence. Severe anxiety and depression. Liver
    damage. Brain damage.
Attorney: Hospitalized?
Me: for brain damage 1989& 1991.
Attorney: Suicidal thoughts?
Me: Yes.
Attorney: Suicidal attempt?
Me: In March 1991.
Attorney: Further symptoms?
Me: Delerium tremens; hallucinations; realistic fantasies;
    memory loss &lapses; confusions; disorientation...
Attorney: OK, OK. Write it all down and come to my office—
    other symptoms, that and limited disabilities, your
    hospitalizations, psychological therapy counseling,
    hospital visits for treatments. Give dates and doctors
    contacted where possible.

Went to the storage/bathroom and checked through my diaries to get together as much information as possible application for Disability to be sent in by the attorney.

Mark

Chapter Twenty Seven

August 18, 1993   Diary to Lauren Morgan

Little work at the office in the morning. In the afternoon, I went to the attorney I had spoken to about applying for Disability. He asked me further questions, with his tape recorder turned on, which I was much better prepared to answer than yesterday.

Attorney: Are you working?
Me: No.
Attorney: Why?
Me: Fired for drinking.
Attorney: Are you able to work?
Me: Nervous, brain damage, distorted thinking, confusion, disorientation.
Attorney: Symptoms in addition to what you mentioned yesterday?
Me: Impaired judgment, paranoid delusions, inability to concentrate, extreme self-consciousness, low self-esteem, feelings of helplessness, lack of control over affairs with inability to cope with everyday problems, nerve-caused eczema, symptoms accompanied by substantially increased blood pressure.

Attorney: Hospitalization?

Me: (1) Asthma—Hospitalized 11/70, 11/88. Treated in Bellevue Chest Clinic as outpatient 11/88-1/89. Dr. C. Aranda.

(2) Arthritis, left knee, army service connected. Hospitalized 3 weeks, Camp Ilmer Hospital, N.J. Feb-March 1954.

(3) Bursitis, left shoulder. Treated V.A. Hospital 5/92. Dr. G. Shore

Attorney: Hospitalizations for Major Disability?

Me: (6/5-7/20/88) for delirium tremens, hallucinations, violent and disoriented behavior.

(1) Rikers Island Mental Observation Ward.

(2) Bellevue Hospital Prison Ward for psychiatric evaluation (2/21-2/22/91) for severe head injury (beating), knife wound (leg).

Bellevue Hospital Center.

(3/91)-exact date not known, but will appear in hospital records) for hallucinations. Bellevue Hospital Center.

(6/24-7/8/91) for detoxification, alcohol dependency, hepatitis. Veterans Administration Hospital Center.

Attorney: Treatments for Major Disability?

Me: (1) Substance Abuse Rehabilitation Program. Veterans Administration Outpatient Rehabilitation Department, 252 Seventh Avenue, New York, N.Y

(July 1991-present) Attended meetings 3 times a week for substance abuse rehabilitation.

(2) Psychological (Individual)Therapy Counseling. Veterans Administration Hospital. Dr. Anthony Biancouiso, Clinical Psychologist.

(August 1991-present) weekly individual therapeutic counseling.

(3) Hospital visits for treatment

(8/15/91; 8/22/91; 10/2/91; 10/15/91; 11/7/91; 11/21/91).

Dr. Frances Sabella—Psychiatrist, Dr. Roger Wolfsohn—Psychiatrist, Dr. William D. Brindle—Psychiatrist.

The attorney asked me further questions I could be asked when interviewed by a Social Security Disability representative and instructed me further in effective answers to give.

Chapter Twenty Eight

Mark questioned himself as to whether or not he could take it if he didn't get back to the apartment. He was tired, uncomfortable, his knees pained him at intervals and he found it difficult to get sleep.

August 18, 1993   Diary to Lauren Morgan

Went after work to competitor discount stock broker firm and punched out stock option quotation on the computer. I had $600 which I had saved from receiving Unemployment Insurance, working and being paid off the books and not paying rent for the storage/bathroom I'm living in temporarily. Intel had seemed to be moving up and the stock chart looked good in an upward trend, plus the Dow Jones Industrial average also seemed to be in an upward trend; so I bought one contract on Intel. At 4 1/8 above the strike price plus a premium of 7/8 brought the price to 5 plus commission, with three weeks to go to expiration of the contract. On this, it seemed I could gain big, or lose big.

Had dinner at the Blarney Stone where one of the girls said I've lost a lot of weight. Went to Al Anon meeting where I got a big surprise—a guy named Murry came over when I was hanging up my coat and said, "I've been looking for you for the three and a half years." He has been dry since. He had a heart attack two years ago; lost a friend from AIDS last spring and his sponsor died about the same time. Was very glad to see him. He's very into Al Anon. Goes to meeting every night. He told me of two celebrities who were big drinkers and Al Anon guys also. Meeting Murry made me feel very good. At another Al Anon meeting where he was a guest speaker, he said his talk was doubly emotional for him as (looking at me while speaking to his audience) he said he met a very dear friend whom he hadn't seen for several years. The good feeling this gave me was rained on when I returned to the storage/ bathroom where Juan came in to wash his hands. He said Elise was having a charge of attempted rape placed against him and he knew I told Erik where he lives. He said the charge of attempted rape by him could not be proven, and if it got to trial and I was called as a witness and told lies, he could come back here and put a bullet in my head. I'm getting a hand gun, which I won't hesitate to use if I have to on this monster.

Mark

August 19, 1993   Diary to Lauren Morgan

Tired as didn't get to sleep until 3:00 a.m. and woke up around 5:30 a.m. Knees feel better, probably because of more compatible weather. Felt lonely and depressed—got to thinking vodka could ease this, but I know it's not the answer and cold put me down for good. Nagging depression about Lauren and what she will do. Was reading "Living Sober" to take my mind off my worries, when a five-year-old girl came into the storage room. She was thin and said she had been left alone and not fed. She told me her name was Africa. I got her something to eat and went to see Rick.

Chapter Twenty Nine

After Mark went to see Rick about five-year-old Africa, Rick investigated and found out that the child was out of one of the small rooms on the top floor front area that was occupied by a colored man in his thirties named Malcolm Sagydoro, who was single. After the room had been rented to Malcolm, he had lived there quietly for some considerable time when a colored woman, in her thirties, called Daisy Dafyurtlu, married, but not living with her husband and the mother of Africa, visited Malcolm a few times, and then with Africa began to sleep and live with Malcolm in the small single room.

When it was brought to Malcolm's attention that it was against the law for the three of them to live in such a small single room, he said he would make this clear to Daisy and she would be leaving. Daisy left for a short time and then came back to living together with Malcom, who when not under her troublemaking influence, had seemed to be a quiet guy who had kept pretty much to himself.

In the small room next to Malcolm's was another small room occupied by a colored fellow in his early twenties named Kevin Loxton, who said there were times when Malcolm and Daisy went out and left Africa with him; and Africa had slept with him nights when Daisy and Malcolm were out all night.

Sometimes when Malcolm and Daisy had wanted to go out, and Kevin was out, they had left Africa alone in the room with the door unlocked. It was on one of such occasion that Africa had walked out of the room and to Mark saying she had been left alone and not fed.

Daisy had had acquaintances come up to see her whom she met in the storage room when Mark was not there. The language used between Daisy and someone visiting her was not just swearing it was downright dirty with words like "mother fucker". Once when Mark was coming up the stairs, he saw Daisy sitting on the lap of a man different than Malcolm, with the fellow saying to her, "Don't touch me." When Rick was told of this, he told Daisy the area was not to be used as a gathering place and she, who did not live in the building, was to leave the premises.

A few days later, Daisy brought to the area a guy named Jason who was said to be her brother, to visit with Malcolm. It seems that Jason decided to look around the building and on to a roof reached by going through the open window of a large bathroom with tub on the floor below that on which Mark was living. Jason had gone on the roof and was sitting there when Inga, a woman in her late twenties, not knowing he was on the roof outside that bathroom, had gone in to use the bathroom and was on the toilet seat when Jason left the roof by climbing through the window into the bathroom. He flashed a knife, walked to and held it at Inga's throat and attempted to rape her. She pleaded with him to please leave her alone, said he could have her money and gave him the money she had in her purse. There was a struggle in which Inga opened the bath room door and screamed, at which time Jason fled down the stairs. Inga lay screaming on the hall floor outside the bathroom door. She was so shaken it was some time before she could stop screaming and compose herself enough to tell what had happened.

Part of Inga's description was that her attacker was colored, tall with slightly slanted eyes and skin of the same shade as Daisy's. Inga also described the clothing her attacker wore, said he had an Afro hair-do and that she had seen him pass previously as a visitor to Daisy and Malcolm. Another tenant, hearing Inga's description of her attacker, said he had seen that person visiting Daisy and Malcolm earlier and that they called him Jason and he had heard Daisy say Jason was her brother.

The police were called in. Police Officer Nicholas made out a report from information given by Inga. When Police Officer Nicholas and another Police Officer talked to Daisy and Malcolm, Daisy said Inga was "a mother-fucking liar." When police asked Daisy what Jason's last name was she said she didn't know (although a tenant had heard her say earlier that Jason was her brother.) When asked where Jason lived, Daisy said she didn't know. The police instructed Daisy to get in touch with Jason and tell him to report to the police station at west 35th Street & 9th Avenue or detectives were going to go out looking for him.

After the police left Daisy, they said about her," She's a bad person. I deal with a lot of people and she's a bad person." Rick said he would see to it, after they had obtained all the information they could from Daisy, that she would be prevented from coming there again.

Malcolm was told that if he allowed Daisy to visit him there, he would be forced to vacate the room.

On the following evening, Inga was stopped on her way home from work at the front entrance to the building by Daisy, who was waiting. "I am going to get you. I am going to get you, you bitch. I am going to get you good, you mother-fucker." Inga, deciding not to go into the building and up to her room, went into the nearest store, a restaurant in the building, and phoned for the police, who came and escorted Inga to her room.

Rick had forms quickly drawn up to take Malcolm and Daisy to court. He went to Daisy and Malcolm to read the charges to be filed against them—threatening to do bodily harm, living there illegally, aiding and abetting an attempted rape suspect, abandoning a five-year-old child.

When Daisy realized that Africa could be taken from her if it went to court, and that her brother as well as she and Malcolm could face time in prison, she and Malcolm agreed to leave if the charges were dropped.

They left that day.

Chapter Thirty

Mark's probation officer contacted him to say he was going on vacation and Mark would have a new probation officer. He also said he talked to Lauren and she said she didn't think there was any chance of her and Mark getting back together, but he added that from the way she said it, he wasn't sure if she meant it. Nor was Mark sure about this probation officer's hedging on what Lauren had said to him.

August 20, 1993   Diary to Lauren Morgan

Went to discount stock broker to check on my stock option and found it was down a point, meaning the $500 I paid was now worth about $400. Will let it ride.

Went to see my son. Feel bad going to see him in my condition. If I didn't feel he had a deep need for me, I wouldn't go. I'm broken up after visits with him.

When I got back to the storage room I occupy, I found my wash cloth in filthy condition, as if someone had washed the tub with it. Also looked as if someone had tried on a pair of my jeans and thrown them over the bathtub.

Feel angry about constant walking around and being resented in this building for hanging around in storage room. I don't blame them; it's a nuisance. Can't help but feel angry about Lauren having the apartment with all the comforts that I should also have with my aching knees and tired feet. Al Anon meetings beginning to bore me. Very bored, angry, lonely and depressed and Lauren hasn't the slightest idea of what it's like to live this frightful way. Absolutely no privacy here and even in the Blarney Stone, people keep asking questions about how I'm doing. Am very disgusted with everything, Lauren and myself. I'm getting very annoyed at her complacency. Feeling numb, which dulls the worry and pain. Going to bed only comfort, if can avoid nightmare.

Chapter Thirty One

Sellner LeMay called Lauren and invited here out for a Saturday night. She accepted. It started at El Flamingo at 21st Street and 10th Avenue. As they entered, Sellner, aware of "Shot Caller" resonating in the background, was greeted by Hal Dubois, one of the frequent patrons. DuBois had one of his hands around a Monte Crisco cigar and the other around a glass of champagne. He put the near empty champagne glass aside and danced with a scantily clad young woman he seemed to know from somewhere.

Sellner and Lauren seemed to gravitate into the dancing on the floor, about as big as a good size living room, oblivious of the sweat others around them were working up. At the end of the dance, they each had a drink of champagne. Then they left this night spot for another night spot, the Tunnel, where they enjoyed Southern food mixed with sounds of rap and reggae. Under blinding lights, women in Versace and men in baggy pants gyrated to the last rap mixes and sipped champagne. Rap followers, mostly black and Latino with white and Asians, danced and drank their cares away. After that, Sellner and Lauren visited other clubs devoted to hip hop culture and rap music.

The latter part of the outing saw them at a restaurant eating some exotic Indonesian food. "There's a lot of money to be made in the substantial underground hip hop network—rap deejay and dance competitions," Sellner told Lauren. "It's not all bad, the violence, as they say. Large clubs pull in $150,000 to $175,000 on rap nights from the door and bar. Smaller places easily pull in $2,000 to $20,000 a night."

"Get much of rowdy crowds?" Lauren asked.

"Fear of that has reduced a number of places to large with maximum security."

"There seemed to be more men than women."

"They outnumber women about three to one. At a few places, patrons are met at the door with metal detectors and burly guards for pat-downs—breasts and buttocks included, some almost strip-searched."

"You seem like someone who has done his homework."

"When you get into this, you don't just have rap artists; you get your own recording company for your rap artists, you get your own television station as a main outlet for your artists' records and tapes, you get your own motion picture studio. You cover as many bases as you can."

"Owner of a night club?"

"Half owner. Thinking about more, not a house of prostitution though, although, there's a hell of a demand for it."

"You're a hustler all right."

"Involved with break dancers, all part of the mix."

"What did you major in in college?" she asked.

"History. If you want to know what's going to happen, just look up and recognize the part of history that's repeating itself."

On the way home to Lauren's place, by stretch limo, Lauren said, "I'm glad they didn't strip-search me at any of the places we were at tonight."

"They do it because of the gangsta thug role, which has set rap back. One club was shut down because a bouncer was shot to death by a club-goer who was refused entry. But it doesn't stop utter rap enthusiasts from rubbing shoulders with celebrity enthusiasts. Some deejays make up to $5,000 a night spinning rap pieces. Some consider attendance or work at these clubs as a springboards for helpful contacts and stardom."

"I'd be more respective of rap if all the 'Godfather' identification was turned off."

"They're working on it. Some gospel artists have enlisted rap to praise the Lord. Rhymed storytelling, backed with rhythmic, electronic produced beats is being absorbed into almost all genres of popular music."

"I like the inclusion of break-dancing."

"Except when praising the Lord. Trying to get the congregation to doing break-dancing could present a problem."

"Ha ha."

"It's included in hip hop though as powerful amalgam of black American and Caribbean cultures. The climate of hip hop is always changing. Powerful poetry often lurks between the music—fluid and reinventing itself—successful collaboration between rap and pop artists. Rap isn't always cannibalizing from them."

As the stretch limo reached Lauren's apartment she said, "I suppose I'll feel guilty if, after having been swept off my feet by you, I don't invite you in."

"I wouldn't object if you did."

"All I can offer you tonight is a soft drink."

"Good enough."

They made their way to Lauren's apartment.

"You have a nice place here."

"It has deteriorated," she said while taking cokes out of the fridge for him and herself. After the drinks were opened and poured in glasses, she showed him around the rest of the apartment including the room Mark had used, which had some of his clothes still in it.

"Some of your boyfriend's clothes still here?" LeMay asked.

"Yes, he hasn't got a large enough place to take them all yet."

"Does he see you often?"

"The intervals between our seeing each other keep getting longer."

"I notice you looking at your watch," he said. "Consider me on my way out. He kissed her hands and was about to kiss her on the cheek when she offered her lips. It was not a long, nor a short kiss, and he didn't part his lips, for which she was grateful.

Chapter Thirty Two

Mark was loaned by Lauren "Women Who Love Too Much," which he read part of. Lauren had underlined appropriate phrases and passages as she had read the book. Mark could identify with some of it with Lauren and himself.

August 23, 1993   Diary to Lauren Morgan

I think Lauren Morgan is confused right now and doubt if she can make any emotional decisions rationally. Feel anxiety about the future—Lauren, my son, apartment, room, stock market, job, court order…Much could have been avoided if I had stopped drinking in May, but who knows…I would not have quit drinking I'm sure at that time; maybe controlled it a little and held on to job and apartment. Hard to tell. At least, now I'm sober for 50 days, which would never have happened by itself. Made my mind transference contact with Lauren and asked if I could come there. She seemed strange and cautious and indicated she wanted to be alone. I got annoyed. When I got back to storage room, had to wait while one of the fellows in the front room of my floor took a bath. Walked to Grand Central Station and to Blarney Stone bar. The attorney who helped me with my application for Social Security Disability was there. Got to talking to him about Lauren. "Can you classify her as your best friend?" he asked. While I stopped to think he added, "You have to think about it. I have a dog that I insisted on keeping when my ex-wife wanted me to give it up. Your wife, lover, son, daughter, sister, brother, father, mother may turn against you, but the one, unselfish better half a man can have in this selfish world is…"

"I can guess—a dog."

"When all others desert you," he went on, "he remains and when you're gone he'll lie on your grave for days. Can you say your girlfriend would do that?" I could only say, "But you should have seen her the first time I saw her, and the first time I saw her in her underwear—wow!" He said, "You want to relieve the highlights you've experienced with this woman. She isn't the girl you knew then and neither are you the guy that knew her then."

Chapter Thirty Three

Mark's mother-in-law who had wondered if her daughter, Sandra, could be taught to be her former sweet, gentle self, had Sandra registered at a finishing school for ladies.

Among classes Sandra attended was one on how to sit properly with a dress on when facing others. An attractive instructress seated in a chair facing a group of girls and women, including Sandra, said, "How we sit with a dress on facing others, particularly men, is important, particularly the part about keeping our legs together. In the short skirts worn today, it's often necessary to cross our legs when sitting down. In our intense interest in something though, we can forget to keep our legs crossed or together so our legs find themselves drifting apart, like this." Here the instructress parted her legs so the crotch of her panties could be seen—and then moved her legs together again.

One of the young girls admitted that she now found herself sexually aroused more than ever.

The instructress commented, "You and the other young teenagers here are at an age when your sex hormones are raging, so you feel you need to find relief in sex."

One of the young girls confessed, "For me, it's self sex since I don't want to get pregnant yet."

The instructress added, "For those of you who feel you must have real sex, insist, it goes without saying, on the use of a condom even if you think it doesn't feel as good."

One of the girls asked the instructress if she thought there had to be love in marriage.

The instructress's answer was, "Someone with character and abilities that promise security can be a good substitute for love."

One of the girls asked, "Can you look on good sex as insurance against a mate's infidelity?"

The instructress said, "Too much of anything, including that, can bring on a sameness bordering on boredom."

One of the girls expressed that if she felt a spouse has to have a mistress she could allow herself enough flexibility to be her husband's mistress so he wouldn't be looking elsewhere for oral sex.

"Give us a demonstration," said one of the girls to the instructress, "of how to get out of a taxi so everybody around you won't see what kind of underwear you're wearing."

"Assuming you'll be wearing underwear," Sandra added, drawing some restrained laughter.

"Before I forget," the instructress said, "I want to mention we have a choral club."

"What kind of a choral club? A girl asked.

"A choral club where loudness is sacrificed for beauty."

"How do you sacrifice loudness where opera is concerned?" a girl asked.

"Which reminds me," said the instructress, "opera lectures are given here with musical excerpts as well as the background and story of the opera to be presented at the "Met" the following week, offering an opportunity for you to impress whomever you may be going to the opera with."

"Fine music has the power to make plants and flowers grow," added one of the girls.

"We, here, have instructions in the fine art of Japanese flower arrangement, a prerequisite for which is the bringing of your own flowers."

One of the girls said she liked swimming, to which the instructress added that they had instructions on advanced swimming, a prerequisite for which is the taking of a shower.

One of the girls said she wanted to act.

"We're all actors," said the instructress. "Our goal is to produce role models, keeping in mind that keeping up with the time doesn't mean we forget there was a time when you could watch a movie with a child and not worry about four-letter words or characters on the screen not keeping their clothes on or someone making a comment to another going out, such as 'have a naughty time.'"

Chapter Thirty Four

August 26, 1993   Diary to Lauren Morgan

Lauren, in mind transference mode, contacted me at the office. Says I can't come back to live there for good as she feels only compassion (a feeling of deep sympathy for another's suffering or misfortune) for me. Not in good shape to work physically. Loss of weight not good. Arms too thin. Went to AA meeting. Didn't like big woman speaker—obnoxious type—probably terrible when drinking. Feel like scared dead-beat. Somebody at Blarney Stone remarked I looked like a lost soul. I must give off the impression of sadness. Another attorney I know who goes there asked me how my visits to Lauren are working out. I said it looks like they aren't. He said, "When a thing's finished, it's finished." Easy to say when you've never been madly in love and so sensitively bonded with someone as to have mental telepathy communication ability between each other (something very few have experienced). He added, "When a woman is taking over your thoughts night and day, you're addicted to her. You're addicted to this woman as surely as if she were a drug, which is making you ill." I had no answer for him. He added, "Look at it this way, the pickings are quite slim for widowed and divorced women. There's a shortage of good men who are considered prime marriage suspects. As most of the available single men in that group are either divorced dads who see their kids on weekends or homos, it means when a woman finds a well-adjusted single guy who she wants to marry, she'll have second thoughts about it. After all, as she gets older, the odds decrease that she'll find a decent guy to marry since men don't live as long. There're fewer to choose from as time goes on. Sometimes there's a prenuptial agreement some women with money are willing to sign, looking at it as an investment."

"What about romance?" I asked. "That's for kids in school who get to thinking of marriage as a fairy tale of some kind. Marriage is just a partnership; like if you own a business, you don't have people work for you because you have fallen in love with them. You have them because you think they're the best under the circumstances for the job you have for them. In taking a wife, do the same—get one whose wants are not too extravagant that'll do the best job for you."

August 27, 1993   Diary to Lauren Morgan

At work, boss paid me a couple of hundred dollars off the books for past recent efforts. During the day, I contacted Lauren in mind transference mode asking if I could come to the apartment. She was hesitant. Told her my knees were aching badly, my mind was numb and had no energy, nor vitality. She communicated she could make out a pale, vague, shadowy, ghostly impression of me and asked if I could make out any such transference impression of her. I could not. It seems in this strong bond between us, she's more sensitive to the mind transference part than I. She reluctantly agreed to let me come to the apartment. Went there after work. Little urge to talk. Felt tired. Cats seemed complacent towards me. Love to be home in this apartment and comfortable. Not much energy for conversation with Lauren. Content to just be with her. Waiting for things to happen. Wonder if I have done all I can for the present and if any possibility of getting back to the apartment with her on a sustained basis. Afraid of what might happen to my stuff and cats if something happens to Lauren.

Chapter Thirty Five

After a restful night in the apartment, Mark got up and fed the cats. While drinking a second cup of coffee, he was aware of Lauren getting up, taking a shower and dressing in a nice sporting outfit. She went out with a filled tote bag—Mark assuming she would be back in a few hours.

Lauren walked a block and met LeMay, waiting in a convertible Cadillac. They had planned this weekend together, away to Saratoga. The weather was great, the ride smooth, the scenery from the New Jersey side of the Hudson impressive. Speeding along the throughway they bypassed Albany and entered Saratoga, nestled in the southern foothills of New York's Adirondack mountains. In this playground, they were ready for a day of unforgettable racing with its gathering of world-renowned thoroughbreds.

From the variety of dining experiences the Saratoga Race Course offered, they went on a sumptuous buffet at the "At the Rail Pavilion," before experiencing the thunder of horses exploding out of the starting gate, hoofs fleeing to the Clubhouse turn while crowds cheered, flying down the backstretch, approaching the far turn, with the crowd's roar becoming almost deafening as down the last stretch, racing horses came going all out to the finish line.

Some won while others hoped for a win to come. LeMay bet heavily after giving Lauren $300 to bet as she wished. He made all kinds of bet in addition to a horse to win, like the exacta (picking the first and second place horse in the exact order), and the trifecta (piking the first three horses in the exact order). In most cases, LeMay bet on the jockey.

"Why do you bet on the jockey?" Lauren asked.

"Owners want the best jock they can find and the best jocks will hardly consider less than the best."

From the race track, they made their way to and sat down to dinner at one of the hundreds of the restaurants serving drinks and everything, from French cuisine to perfect after-dinner coffee. LeMay had made about $8,000 at the races. Lauren, who had bet on horses she liked the physical appearance of, lost all LeMay had given her to bet. "I'm sorry," she said.

"Nonsense," LeMay told her. "There's plenty more where that came from, thanks to the world of rap."

"Is it hard to get into?"

"A lot of people think it is easy to get into. It takes a lot of perseverance and lot of heart and selling, after you have the talent to make it. A beginner rapper starts shopping a homemade demo tape. Your average successful rapper is in his early twenties, married, has a child and earns a hundred thousand or so a year with an album under his belt."

"Likely thinking of his next album and the next."

"Aware of different strokes for different folks with rappers rhythms and messages, seeking what will take—ego trio raps, gospel raps, party time raps, comedy raps, political raps, every type of rap."

"Talking about anything in life?"

"To a beat and keeping it simple:

'If your woman steps out with another man,
That's the breaks, that's the breaks,
And she runs off with him to Japan,
That's the breaks, that's the breaks."'

"You feel something new in rap is needed?"

"Something new is always needed—emotional rhythm and words that are universal. I check in at places like Club 28 looking for anything commercially new. If you want something new, go underground in a quirky confluence of cultures. By the time it gets to Broadway, if it should, it's not new. I'm always searching for a different kind of beat. For a record, produced by a major label, to break even it typically must sell 80,000 to 100,000 discs."

"Usually that doesn't happen?"

"But every once in a while, a hit comes along and you can get a hit that sells five million copies. With an estimated return of $10 a disc to the record company that's $5,000,000 spawned by a $1,000,000 up front investment of that disc. New artists are typically able to negotiate a 10% to 12% cut, and they only get that after the record company, the producer and everybody else is paid back."

"A new rapper has to have sold 80,000 to 100,000 discs or he makes nothing?"

"Close to that."

After their meal, they took in a performance by the New York City Ballet at the Saratoga Performing Arts Center. "Quite a foil for rap," Lauren commented.

"There are after all other things in life besides rap," he added.

From the Ballet, they stopped at the sidewalk café for wine, followed by espresso coffee before making their way to one of the charmingly exclusive motels.

Alone in a room in the motel he kissed her hands. "Know what I feel like doing?"

"Don't keep me guessing."

"Taking a shower."

"I too, after you," she said.

"I guess you're not the sort who has to have the lights turned out when you're undressing, he said. "Watching you undress is part of the foreplay."

"The foreplay begins when a couple first meet."

"I have in my brief case some new pairs of silk panties you would look good in."

"Did you think I might forget to bring mine?"

"It's just that, I'd like to see you in them after you take your shower."

"And dry myself," she added as she made her way to the shower.

He continued undressing while she took a shower in the same room with double beds. When she had finished her shower, he took his shower while she dried herself and put on a pair of the silk panties.

He came out of the shower with a towel around his waist and sat on one of the double beds watching her saying, "As I've imagined you this way in my dreams, only better."

"I want to thank you for the double bed arrangement," she got into one of them and rolled over.

"You're welcome," he said as he rolled over in the other bed.

The following mid-morning, Lauren heard LeMay saying, "Rise and shine," to which she said, "You gave me an idea for a rap piece."

"How?"

"Could mention being thankful I don't have you turn your back when I'm undressing, or request you shut yourself in a closet, or me shut myself in a closet while I'm undressing…"

"Thanks for the idea."

"It's really yours."

"Thanks for letting me know I gave myself an idea."

After breakfast at the nearest restaurant, they strolled through the town with its treasure trove of shops, picking up gifts for Lauren. Then they experienced what was said to be the ultimate in rest and relaxation submerged in a soaking mineral bath, followed by a massage by professionals.

Following this, they drove around the surrounding countryside with its beautiful waterways, farms and historical sights. And they sipped champagne at a polo match before heading back to New York City. The ride along the throughways was swift and then it was a matter of making your way to and under the Hudson and to the front of the building Lauren lived in. LeMay knew how to show a girl a good time. Lauren was swept off her feet.

She went into her apartment alone. Mark, a bundle of nerves, was there waiting. "When you went out Saturday morning," he said, "I assumed you would be back in a couple of hours. When you didn't return through the day, I got worried. Then I figured, you might be back in the middle of the night. I couldn't sleep. I kept looking at the clock. I drank about a dozen coffees through the night getting increasingly worried. In the morning, I was progressively worried and depressed. I didn't know what to do. I wondered if I should call the police, but I didn't, remembering you had a restraining order, meaning I shouldn't be here."

"I'm glad you didn't," Lauren said, noticeable disheveled.

"I'm worried sick."

"I'm sorry."

"Where did you go?"

"Saratoga."

"Who with?"

"Sellner LeMay, a guy I've known for a while. He's six feet three inches, lean and in his thirties, dark, quite handsome and had lots of money.

"Into drugs?"

"Into rap. He handles rap artists and a lot of interests revolving around that."

"At least you're not hurt. If anything happened to you, I don't think I could take it."

Chapter Thirty Six

Mark shaved, showered, fed the cats and went to the storage room where Rick told him Neil said he thought he would move out that week.

August 30, 1993   Diary to Lauren Morgan

In the evening, went to an Al Anon meeting. Lately, am conscious of the necessity of attending 90 meetings in 90 days. Am only 11 behind now and can make it up if I want. Attended two Al Anon meetings today. After last meeting, a girl talked about her problems to me in the street for fifteen minutes and went into sobbing. Some passers-by looked at me as if I'm a woman harasser. Went to storage room feeling numb. Go to court Wednesday, fearful of what might happen. I think I have blanketed all my feelings and shrunk my personality. Afraid—have confidence. Dislike myself. Trying to hide fear. Sleep helps if I can get it.

August 31, 1993   Diary to Lauren Morgan

Thought about Unemployment Insurance form I filled out and mailed. On the form where I asked if I was trying for a job, I wrote, "In jail, at Riker's, first half of July." This may cause me to lose 3 weeks checks or lose rest of payments for 6 months. Am having a devastating emotional blow which floors me with extreme self-loathing for stupidity. Terrible attack of mental and emotional anxiety, as there's nothing I can do but worry. Try to convince myself it's useless to worry about something I can't do anything about, but still the trauma. Trying to think of possible solution if Unemployment Insurance people question me about jail. Could say it was at my request because Lauren had put me out of our apartment and I had no place to stay. But what if Unemployment Insurance checks this out? Doubt they will, because with the cost cutting, they haven't got the staff to check. This thought doesn't help my emotional pain. Why am I so stupid? Have thoughts maybe a little drink would ease my pain but these are thoughts I have to smother. 59 days sober; but feeling miserable and depressed. Beth said she heard from the inside of her room someone trying the lock to her room. Said she also heard someone trying to break into Neil's room, which is the room I'm waiting for Neil to move out of if he hasn't already done so. Depressing thought. It's 9:15 pm and Juan has been at the sink twice giving me hateful stares; he'll do anything for money, which he always seems to be out of. Warren has gone to the bathroom downstairs to wash because of me being here. I feel uneasy and think they resent me being here when they have a right to use this in private. Read more of "Women Who Love Too Much," still finding parallels between book and me and Lauren. I think Lauren has used some or a lot of the book's logic about getting outside help and helping herself and not bothering with me. It shows in her attitude towards me. Maybe I better not pressure her too much about going back to her apartment for good until I can improve myself mentally, physically and financially.

Chapter Thirty Seven

September 1, 1993   Diary to Lauren Morgan

Went to court. I was in the first case and (am ready for this) it's postponed until some time in October because no probation report in file. At noon, met attorney at Blarney Stone drinking vodkas. He asked if I was back with Lauren. "Not fully," I said. He told me he has a client whose wife is ready to sue for him for being a lousy lover. "She says there's no excuse for her husband being as lousy at sex as he is. Says she has already spent years trying to teach him how to please her in bed." I asked, "Does her husband not have the energy, which I can identify with?"

"She said her husband failed dismally when he tried to turn her on. Did they try sex counseling? She said she bought her husband sex manuals but he wouldn't read them, his idea of love not being having sex with a manual in one hand and his wife in the other. She said her husband's idea of sex was a two-minute tussle and rolling over and going to sleep. He had no concept of foreplay, no expressions of tenderness. She thought, when her husband didn't perform before they were married it was because he was innocent and would improve after they were married. After his failure to improve, she got so frustrated she finally consulted an attorney, wanting to sue her husband for years of cheating her of her reasonable marital rights. The case has not been put before a judge yet because this woman, her husband, and I agreed her husband would make a focused and exerted attempt to shape up between the sheets." Women have come a long way.

September 5, 1993   Diary to Lauren Morgan

Little work to do at office on Friday, where I received mind transference from Lauren saying an Unemployment check had arrived for me. Met her at Blarney Stone after work. Bought her a couple of drinks. I had a soft drink. We took subway to her apartment. Watched part of "Women in Love" and had coffee. Felt tired and listless. Went to bed early.

Had coffee and back to bed. Lauren drinking beer most of day. She made stew which was very good. To bed early.

Up earlier today at apartment. Napping, still tired. Lauren's attitude changing—more affectionate with her beer and scotch. Feel uneasy and afraid of something—the uncertainty of my life and self-hate. Don't like to think about leaving apartment but feel I accomplish nothing here—just sleep, rest, eat, watch TV junk. Little conversation. Thought of going to Al Anon meeting near apartment but didn't go, telling myself I need physical rest more, although I'm trying to make 90 meetings attended in 90 days of non-drinking. I think reason for some idea, I'll have guilt feelings if I don't make 90 meetings attended in 90 days is that after that, I have an excuse to attend considerably fewer meetings. Am not sure about going deep into Al Anon work and reading Big book, getting sponsor, etc. Realization against going to AA meetings consistently afterwards is that I can read Big book (which I still need to obtain).

September 6, 1993   Diary to Lauren Morgan

Watched TV and read on this Labor Day holiday. Lauren drinking beer and scotch, feeling a little giddy and affectionate. Willing to discuss my living at apartment when she goes home at Christmas. After a nice dinner, Lauren got dressed up and went out alone. Her mood swings confuse me. Here today, she had seemed more loving and willing to discuss my living in the apartment when she goes home at Christmas, and then after dinner, I notice her getting dressed up to go out alone. Didn't tell me where she was going. As I didn't want to start what might have been another skirmish, I tried to act not too concerned. A couple of hours later, she came not too steady on her feet, and went to bed with the two cats.

September 7, 1993   Diary to Lauren Morgan

Up early, fed cats and left apartment. Feel physically and mentally improved because of rest and food and vitamins at the apartment, but hurtfully confused with Lauren's manner. At noon, stopped in to discount stock brokerage firm and punched out stock quotes on the computer, including the stock option I have. It's back to even now. Hope to have some more money soon to buy another stock option. After work, went to Al Anon meeting. A colored fellow there, in his forties, with lots of confidence, said everything is told in the Big book (maybe I should read it). He was robust, good natured, nice to be with, and showed me a poem called "How Come":

> When I was born, I was black;
> When I grew up, I was black;
> When I was sick, I'm black;
> When I go out into the sun, I'm black.
> But you:

When you were born, you were pink;
When you grow up, you are white;
When you get sick, you are green;
When you go out in the sun, you are red;
When you die, you turn purple.
And you called me colored?"

Mark was told by Beth that Rick said, Neil had left the room he had occupied, which was to be cleaned. Mark looked at the room with Rick and the bed was taken out. Part of the walls would need to be plastered and the room painted, windows cleaned and new linoleum or rug put down.

September 8, 1993   Diary to Lauren Morgan

When room is ready, wonder if big white bench in storage room can be moved in and used as a bed/couch. Look forward to being able to read and sleep in private. Can slowly bring my things from the apartment. Must be thrifty. Must save $ to protect myself. Must not drink, although at present don't see a problem, although I'm may be underestimating the subtlety of alcoholism. Must try hard not to get complacent at work, as seem to be falling into this pattern at least in attitude and taking 1 ½ hours for lunch and leaving early and dressing casually. Must get job back with full pay instead of receiving meager payment off the books. Unemployment still unsure (stupid admittance by myself of 3 weeks in jail may come up on 9/17 when I go there). If I do get my regular job back, must resist my frustrations and annoyances and not let them interfere with work. The storage room is accumulating things again—old chairs, busted TV set, bags, clothes hanging on rack. Can't wait to get into clean and private room. Feel blank and vacant but not depressed. Just unsure of things and uneasy about my lack of self-confidence & assuredness. I feel like I am, without alcohol, weak and unassertive as well as afraid of circumstances and people. Can this possibly change? I think this present state of mind and attitude is what I despise in myself and what I have been trying for all these years to conceal with alcohol—which I don't have the support of now.

September 10, 1993   Diary to Lauren Morgan

At work, pulled report lists, checked clearances and finished report lists. Left early. Stopped off at a discount stock brokerage firm and found my stock option was up a point above what I paid for it. This and getting out of the storage/bathroom into a small room for myself might be omen of better things to come. Realize now though, I'll have to pay rent, which will leave me with not as much to invest in the stock market. 67 days dry. Told this at Al Anon meeting. Voice felt higher than usual with fear. Thought maybe Cindy noticed it—she always has a half smile. Boss didn't pay me anything off the books for the week—probably forgot. I hate being in this position—can't ask him because I'm supposed to be working for nothing; but I'm sure he meant to pay me. Meanwhile I won't know 'til next week, it being on my mind over the weekend. Contacted Lauren and asked to come to apartment. She said OK. Had to wait for her at front of apartment (only she has the keys). Did almost nothing all evening except buy sandwiches to eat. Tired. To bed early.

Chapter Thirty Eight

Mark had a dream during the night seeming to call up some early years.

September 11, 1993   Diary to Lauren Morgan

In nightly dream is my oldest brother, Peter, a couple of years older, who I idolized. The dream begins with a grouping around a celebrated actor, Clark Gable, who goes over and shakes hands with my big brother, Peter. I am lagging a few steps behind Peter, in his shadow so to speak, feeling I'm not really noticed, with everyone paying attention to Clark and Peter. Then Peter introduces Clark to me. I buy them lunch. I liked to have people believe I was one allowed to be on friendly terms with Clark and Peter, it making me feel important and a big ego booster for me—I wanted as many people as possible to see me with them. I finished eating dinner last, although trying very hard to eat fast to keep up with them (the eating speed possibly being a symbol for success in life). Peter finished almost as fast as Clark. I thought to myself that Peter was respected by the others for just being himself, without any self-conscious feelings or thoughts, whereas, I had to ponder and consider if what I wanted to do was correct and if it would be accepted by the others. I was conscious of only being tolerated at the table because I was Peter's brother, reflecting that it was like that throughout childhood. All through the years I was conscious, envious and hurt by being overlooked because of being Peter's brother. He had the respect which I too wanted and I was painfully aware of the second-class or kid brother treatment.

"You don't have to respect Mark, he's only Peter's kid brother."

In reality, Peter had me do things that he should have done himself. When he was 16, we were staying at the beach with the family for a month and we met a girl of 14 or 15 at the beach and made a date (the three of us) to meet that evening on the beach to watch fireworks. I had to go with him and stay and make conversation all during the fireworks so he wouldn't be having to make conversation all that time by himself.

When he was 13 (I was 10 or 11) he got a paper rout which paid him about $8-$10 a week and he got me to deliver half the route for $1 a week plus giving him all my tips.

Later on, when I was 12 or 13, I got my own paper rout near his high school which I delivered myself (a large route) for a year. While he was in high school and I was in Jr. High, he needed spare money and asked me for half of my paper rout which I gave him. But he made me pick up all the papers after school, split them into my bag and his and carry both bags to where the rout began.

I also recall that if he was threatened verbally or physically, I would always intercede and stand up for him, even if it meant fighting for him despite the difference in age and size.

He continually asked me to do things for him that something prevented him from doing himself, like asking questions of strangers, buying certain things in stores, delivering things.

He knew of my adulation for him and used it because I had got used to doing almost anything then (compared to now). I had no problem about being involved with people for him. Actually, I was much more assertive and pushier for him than I was for myself, and all this to gain and keep his favor.

I recall having to be constantly witty, bold, taking extra risks to show him and others how smart, witty and tough I was, even though smaller and younger. I always had to impress him and our crowd.

All during those years, I used my wit and intelligence to get favor and attention from all so Peter would be proud of me. When Peter entered the Army, I felt I no longer had to be bold for him. I wasn't bold and assertive for myself. Maybe I couldn't be bold and strong for myself because I was only Peter's younger brother and only had stature in relation to him. On my own I was nothing, and why should I be bold and strong when Peter and the gang were no longer there to appreciate and respect me for it?

Chapter Thirty Nine

Mark got up late, fed the cats and drank coffee, noticing Lauren watching a horror movie.

September 12, 1993   Diary to Lauren Morgan

When she talks, sipping rum and beer, it's nonsense, silly... When I showed some discontent, Lauren said she resented me tearing pages out of the telephone directory. I cleared out some of my junk and writing. I began to get depressed going through stuff in my suitcases to take to my new small room. Apprehension about new room being too small for all my belongings. Hard to concentrate—uneasy and worried of new transition (too old to start over now after years of progress in getting all things together in one nice apartment). Angry at myself for gross stupidity. Annoyed that I can't drink normally under pressure on occasion. Went to bed early with the two cats.

September 13, 1993   Diary to Lauren Morgan

Up early, fed cats, packed things of mine to take from apartment to my new small room. At work, boss paid me off the books for last week. Later paid rent to Rick to occupy room vacated by Neil and we moved big white bench in. Still depressed over what I have to look forward to in life. Am confused and think Lauren is, although she wants me to move in this small room (and she can have the whole apartment for herself). Found time during the day to see my son. Back at my new small room, when I was getting ready to go to bed I was curious to see if I could see the red light on the Empire State building from my pillow. Yes I can.

September 14, 1993   Diary to Lauren Morgan

Slept fair after the first night in my small room with the door locked and window open. At work, Henry says the boss is supposed to fire Allotta—maybe enough $ now to pay me full salary. To Blarney Stone in evening where Perez, who was drinking 2 vodkas while I was there) embarrassed me with make-believe hugging and loud talk about me being a man and bad mouthing AL Anon and AA people as morons. Claims I will go back to drinking etc. Not a good influence. Seems to have no direction but drinking—talking about divorce. Drink has a bad hold on him. Says he spent $10,000 in past four months on drinking! Wonder if I appear afraid and shy to people at Blarney Stone. Apprehensive about talking in front of people at AA meetings. Wendy said when she first came to meetings, she also couldn't talk and had no personal control, but it came to her from her higher power. Where's my higher power? I'm only five behind the 90 & 90 schedule. Have to be careful I don't, after I meet my attending 90 AA meetings in 90 days schedule, drop off severely from attending Al Anon meetings and try to handle problem on my own so I go back to drinking, which would be the end. Wish I had Court over with. Am not in frame of mind to bring rest of my belonging from apartment to my small room. Don't know what will happen about spending weekends or part of weekends at apartment now that I have room of my own. Now 11:30pm—listening to Dvorak's 7th Symphony on radio.

Chapter Forty

Lauren and Beth, who had hit it off from when they first met, got together again at Lauren's apartment. Lauren seemed to be trying to do more for herself with counseling and self-discipline. She was making an effort to not drink on working days in the week, but on weekends in a more restrained manner than formerly. Although on the week day that Beth visited her, Lauren made an exception.

Lauren, who was drinking rum and beer, told Beth about meeting LeMay and thought the change was helpful. While mentioning Mark, she added that a reason why she's understanding about Mark visiting her, is partly because "the cats were so crushed at our breakup. They're extremely sensitive. I felt they could grieve themselves into a neurotic state if Mark and I didn't show some sense of being here for them. Somebody who suggested that one cat could go to each of us simply doesn't understand. When Mark is here, he and I go about our lives like boarders in a rooming house. Aside from that, we try in front of the cats to do our best to act as if things are normal. They have a lot more understanding than we give them credit for."

"I'll drink to that," Beth added.

"Which reminds me," said Lauren, "we can also drink to Helen, a girl I met at the bar across the street a few nights ago. Helen had met a guy at a Singles club where she and he got to talking and hit it off right away. She gave the guy her telephone number and he gave her his, which was an out of town number. Helen and the guy went out a couple of times, followed by a night between the sheets. The morning after that, the guy told Helen he was married, but that he and his wife were about to separate. Helen believed him, until later, he said he and his wife had patched things up. Helen felt so humiliated, she later wrote this out of town guy a letter saying she was pregnant—which she was not. Nine months later, Helen sent the guy a picture of a girl-friend's baby with a note saying it was hers and his. Since then, child support checks have been arriving from the guy to Helen."

Chapter Forty One

Mark was trying not to think of all the wasted years of loss of money, security, and job. He could have been independent by now with no money worries. He needed to move the rest of his belongings with Lauren at the apartment's comfortable space to his small room.

September 17, 1993   Diary to Lauren Morgan

Feel blank, lonely, lost. Must keep sober and working and see what may come along to improve present position. Possible stock market trading will do something for me.

Went to Unemployment office. Prayed to God there would be no problem as a result of my having previously told them I was in jail at Rikers Island. Held my breath while girl brought my name up in the computer. Looks like there'll be no problem. As soon as I got relief on this problem, another problem was ready to take its place namely, that Unemployment people may recheck and deny me money sometime in the future. My next worry will be going to court for sentencing for what Lauren has accused me of.

In evening, went to Al Anon meeting where a big, red-headed guy, former athlete, spoke—the kind of guy I would have liked to drink with. After meeting, shook hands with him and asked if he ever went to Billy Budd's. He said he did. I feel drawn toward going back to the bar scene and the comfortable feeling and self-confidence from a drink or so, from talking to him. But put the thought out of my head. The thought of returning to my small room has me feeling it will be too small for all my belongings, many of which are still in the apartment with Lauren. In the mind transference contact with Lauren, I asked if I could come to the apartment. She said OK. Got there around 7:00 pm. Inside, we talked while she sipped rum and beer. I asked if LeMay would be moving in with her.

"He'll come and go," she said.

"He's married?"

"He's separated from, and expected to get a divorce from his wife."

"I still have a chance with you?" I asked.

"I've tried to make things easier for you—letting you come here when I have a restraining order, letting you have a comfortable place to break the monotony of what has been your recent living arrangement."

"With restrictions."

"You don't acknowledge I've tried to make things easier for you?"

"Yes. Do you love this guy LeMay?"

"I recognize he has been considerate and helpful."

"Do you love him like you love me?"

"I don't love you like I loved you."

"You still have some feeling for me?"

"I feel sorry for you," she told me.

September 19, 1993   Diary to Lauren Morgan

Over the weekend, Lauren interpreted my saying little as sulking and threatened—if I was not going to speak to her, I could go back to the room I had moved into. She did not cease sipping beer and rum on both days, while I took boxes of my belongings out of closets and got out sheets, pillow cases, towels, wash cloths, blankets, clothes. Talked to her about coming to the apartment in the middle of the week. She was reluctant, saying she may visit girlfriend in New Jersey, and on Monday night goes to counselor, and on Tuesday night she's thinking of going to women's meeting about abusive men.

September 20, 1993   Diary to Lauren Morgan

Up early, fed cats, cleaned cat box, packed more belongings and left apartment to go to my small room, after which, I went to work where I was not busy. Boss griping at me about nothing. I started to get anxious about whether he forgot to pay me or is just spiting me. I didn't want to ask him for it. Kept my mouth shut. At lunch time, went to discount brokers office and punched out stock quotations on the computer. My option is up $200 above what I paid for it. Having to pay rent now, I won't have as much money to put into the stock market. If my Unemployment Insurance runs out and my Disability Insurance application has not come through, the only income I'll have is what I'm being paid off the books for working for nothing.

While at the second floor, coming up the stairs on the way to my room, I bumped into Sister Amalaina. She is the main wheel in the fortune telling—psychic—astrology set-up, occupying the second floor of the building I live in. She's charmingly attractive and on some days, hires somebody to stand out in front of the building handing out printed sheets in which she advertises herself as God-gifted Sister Superior Amalaina, Saint for Lost Causes, psychic and expert in astrology, horoscopes, past lives, future forecasts and live tarot readings.

She has a husband who acts as an aide to her. He seems good-natured and believing in her superior talents, does what she says. They are gypsies, and much of the time, seem to send out for their meals.

Perhaps, seeing in me a "lost cause" prospective client, she showed me the second floor she and her husband occupy for business and living quarters. In the little room where she does her business, she has a crystal ball on a glitzy table, and from a ceiling with stars is a slow whirling cut-glass globe which has a spot light shining on it so it reflects lights and shadows around the little room, lending an atmosphere of the mysterious, especially when the Sister is wearing her black robe with large and small gold stars scattered around it.

A fellow who had gone in to have his fortune told by Sister Amalaina told me she started off asking for $5.00, which covered little more than her looking into her crystal ball and telling him he had a problem and what his fee would be after the initial $5.00 payment—it being not unlike a carrot being held in front of a donkey in which, the Sister may hold in front of the prospective client universal subjects like love, money, career, health and what life has in store. It's not entirely unlike forecasting the weather where it can be said the weather will be partly cloudy, where you can hardly go wrong. How often do we ever get a completely cloudless day? Or possibly like some can tell if another is an optimist or a pessimist by the a glass of water half way up to the top is described—half full indicating the optimist and half empty indicating the pessimist. In a not somewhat dissimilar manner, I was told that when the Sister is reading you, she can, along the way acquire help from you by gathering what comments you unnoticeably come out with as she proceeds. For instance, when the Sister says she sees a problem in the way of someone known to you, you might say, "Yes Bob…." And the Sister on that trail may add that Bob too has a problem wherein it may be necessary for him to receive the Sister's analysis; which gives the Sister more information to follow up on and so on.

Sister Amalaina says she guarantees to reunite separated loved ones, and when she cannot reunite a separated couple, she'll say it as because they were not loved ones. In digging into your problems, is she possibly trying to take business away from psychologists? Each extra avenue you have answered by the Sister, meaning extra fee, is not unlike a doctor discovering something you need a test for leading to something else you need a test for and so on for as long as your checkbook holds out.

I don't think you need a license to forecast into the future. Some, I guess, just hang up a sign and proceed to ask you for your birthdate, time of birth, birth place and fee.

Chapter Forty Two

Mark was spitting up phlegm. His emotions seemed semi-blank. He was thinking about his court date and probation officer. Worrying him was his going to Lauren's apartment with her approval, which possibly could be stated later by her as not having had her approval, if more serious problematic controversy arose between them.

September 22, 1993   Diary to Lauren Morgan

Have to find out whether I say I've been going to Lauren's apartment on weekends and if this violates court order if she says it's OK. Also, if she could cancel the 3-year probation likely sentence. Also, if I should say I'm working for nothing! At Al Anon meeting, sat with waitress from Blarney Stone who has been on the wagon six months today. Feel ill, like I have fever. At another AA meeting I saw Chris (dark, straight, short hair and glasses) who said to me, "Congratulations on being dry 81 days." She added she has been watching me. I wonder what she meant by "watching me". Maybe she has picked up my self-consciousness. After three AA meetings today, I feel I'm making a small step forward. My shyness could eventually be overcome. I have to keep trying to expose myself to people and try to talk more. People at last AA meeting I attended were somewhat scroungy, unshaven, derelict-looking types-a lot of addicts, maybe mostly cross-addicted alkies. Looks like I'm going to make 90 AA meetings in 90 days dry.

September 26, 1993   Diary to Lauren Morgan

Received mind transfer communication from Lauren at the office on Friday saying she's home with some bad side pains. Went to the apartment in the evening.

Her bad side pains continued yesterday and today. She's sipping rum and beer. I am concerned about her health and her ability to take care of herself, apartment and cats. Don't know what will happen if she gets sick or there's a fire in the apartment. Apprehensive about court and sentence.

September 27, 1993   Diary to Lauren Morgan

Up early, fed cats and left apartment with more of my belongings to take to my small room. At office, Rex told me the boss asked him to move to another location and he thinks he will. This may open up spot for me but not sure and won't speculate on it now. Boss didn't pay me again. It annoys me because I'm never sure whether he remembers or not and it should not have to be on my mind. In the evening, I sat in my room feeling like I'm wasting my time. I seem to be going from Monday through Friday like a robot, just passing time at the office, eating and sleeping until the weekend comes. Lauren just seems to live for today. When I'm there, she just watches TV, smokes, drinks beer and rum and reads sometimes. Now 10:30 pm, listening to a Mozart symphony.

September 29, 1993   Diary to Lauren Morgan

Too much coffee and smoking lately has given me diarrhea. I was bothered at work because the boss has not paid me. I mentioned to him, "I didn't know if you forgot, or if you wanted it that way but you didn't pay me for last week." He got sensitive and said "Aren't I entitled to forget?" I said, "Of course, but I had told you I would work for nothing and I didn't know if you were going to take me up on it, or just forgot to pay me." The matter was dropped. It continued on my mind but I didn't want to bring it up to him again. In the latter part of the morning, I went to NY state job placement office, it being necessary because I am to them Unemployed and receiving Unemployment insurance. Waited an hour and a half to see a well-dressed colored man. I told him, in order to save us time, that I was pretty sure I would be re-hired by my former firm in December, which he wrote up on his form. Went back to office, where boss was unpleasant. Must try to forget about my apprehensive fears and speculations. After work, went to AA meeting. 88th day dry. Still have urge to buy Big book (bible) and get more into the Al Anon spirit; but after I make 90 AA meetings in 90 days dry, I'm still thinking of attending fewer AA meetings with their phrases like, "Thank you for my sobriety," "feel gratitude," "turn it over," "one day at a time," "keep coming," "I can identify with that," etc. may be able to incorporate big book and Al Anon program slowly into a continued method of recovery of my own, not counting on any short cut cure for my weaknesses (self-pity, self-disgust, self-hate, fear, insecurity, inferiority).

October 3, 1993   Diary to Lauren Morgan

After receiving mind contact with Lauren, I met her at the Blarney Stone at 5:00 and went to her apartment with her. I did attend 90 Al Anon meetings in 90 days dry. Congratulations to myself.

At apartment yesterday, I cleaned out kitchen tool drawers and cabinets—now much neater. Nice to get rest, better food.

Today, I slept until noon. I talked to Lauren about rescinding Court order of restraint. She is reluctant, saying there's no violation if she permits my being there. I said I would check with my probation officer.

Chapter Forty Three

October 4, 1993   Diary to Lauren Morgan

Up early, packed bag with sweaters and pants and left apartment. Lauren contacted me at the office in the morning wanting to know if I called my probation officer. Said I would. Called probation officer and asked about my visiting Lauren at apartment on weekends. He says I'm in violation of Court order. To rescind court order, Lauren has to go to court with me this week and judge may still not rescind order if he thinks I might go wacky later on etc. Contacted Lauren later and told her what had been explained to me. She still doesn't want to void court order against me, saying she's not sure if I will relapse and she will have to go through everything again.

Can't help thinking of LeMay. The more I think of him, the more I feel Lauren's not telling me everything. Maybe he's not telling her as much as I think he is. I am disturbed over this. In the sunny light of hope, I find the cold light of reality. No more will be days when we were like innocent young dreamers at play in each other's arms in the sensual sun of a midsummer. While passing a store window that had what seemed like a Thanksgiving scene, it got me to thinking

I and Lauren probably wouldn't be spending holiday seasons together like we used to. I feel depressed; others happiness leading me to gloomily ponder my inner misery, bringing into focus disappointments, utter loneliness and isolations. Good times and celebrations now will alienate me. My disturbed reflections on existence, philosophy and theology confuse me. I don't know if Buddha, Mohammed or Christ were divine or charismatic and tragic individuals who followed their own inner calling and went their own way despite enormous difficulties and often widespread abuse through misunderstanding by others of their motives and ideals.

Questionable is the suggestion religion can be dangerous when it stultifies human effort relying on a supernatural being to cure and rectify ills and evils, and the suggestion we request aid or comfort by prayer over energizing all our effort into pure concentrated force of will to act and if thwarted act again without giving up rather than appealing to an abject fantasy secluded from us whom we know not of but through faith. Where was He when praying Jews by the millions died in Nazi concentration camps in World War II? If I pray, let it not take away from any of an intense will to act.

And there's existential theory in which two of its best known exponents, Kierkegaard and Sartre, are as far apart as are any of the major religions. The existential thinker influenced by the atheistic Sartre, takes on the burden of freedom and responsibility of choice in face of collapsing values, whether religious, philosophical, social or political. It doesn't matter what you do, God or not, believer or atheist, since any individual is only responsible to himself for his actions, good or bad. Only man-made laws govern your choice. It lasts only for a transitory period—one's lifetime.

Kierkegaard represents a Christian faith with few ties to Sartre's theories except the dominant belief in personal freedom. His communication with God is extremely personal, not conforming to any institutionalized religion.

Oriental thought, primarily Hinduism and Buddhism is something else—possibly more appealing—especially the potentialities of Samsara. These eastern philosophies appear to be direct antithesis of Sartre's form. Samsara (roughly reincarnation) without Nirvana (salvation from pain and suffering) is at least a sustaining or prolonging ideology if you think in terms of continuous existence at whatever level.

Does union with God or a transcendental power through belief, mystical insight or philosophical speculation, end with the death of the mortal body? Is there such a thing as transmigration of souls after death? Is living for now and hereafter? If there is no supernatural deity (man, nature, spirit or idea) is a life of goodness and piety (except for its own sake) wasted? Are there in the words of Camus, "…no longer guilty men, only responsible ones"?

If by Sartre's existential theory that man is a transient bubble on the surface of existence that emerges for an instant of world time and fades and will never be again, or Kierkegaard's personal mystical union with his God and a reward in heaven; or by Eastern theology, that man's soul will assume a new material body after death, is there any credible doctrine of continuity of being, material or spiritual, to justify anything but temporal and expedient thought and action? If you do good, noble and humanitarian deeds now, is there a reward later, or as the saying goes is virtue its own reward? If you lead a life of evil, is punishment and perdition your destiny after death?

A mystic seeks to attain a spiritual state where there is no belief and disbelief—only absolute and pure sensation, ecstasy and union with a Universal Almighty, probably not for anyone, but a soul possessing the most exalted and keenest sensitivity.

There's probably some great Architect of the Universe somewhere keeping the planets in their orbits, the earth turning on its axis around the sun, the moon around the earth, galaxies from running into each other—a sense of order in space. For those who think that's proof, there's belief—for those that don't, there's doubt. I'm like a tennis ball going back and forth in the court of one and the other.

Chapter Forty Four

October 5, 1993   Diary to Lauren Morgan

Could be possible, if I go to apartment and the authorities check and find me there, I could be charged with breaking a Court order, even though Lauren gave permission for me to be there. Will I have to stay away from the apartment? Very annoying. Everything going wrong. Angry about maybe having to stay in my little room, instead of going to apartment on weekends. I almost hate Lauren. Can't make up her idiot mind. I should try not to talk to her but I need clothes of mine and other things from the apartment.

Went to AA meeting where I was told I'll be given a 90-day coin for 90 days dry. Speaker was good, talking about several infidelities. Glad I went to meeting because I don't want to get into the habit of not going. Made half-hearted attempt to buy big book. Seem to be going about a little of a step at a time. Will I develop into going from my room to the office and back and to AA meetings and back to my little room? Must have some place else to go and something else to do.

October 6, 1993   Diary to Lauren Morgan

To court this morning where I went before the judge, I received a 3-year probation sentence. Saw woman probation officer after. Will report once a month for a while and then every 2 months and if everything OK, they could terminate probation after one year. Must get signed letter from AA group every 3 months about regular attendance there; and I may have to go to a hospital for alcoholic counseling.

Have chest cold which is getting worse. Went to AA meeting where a guy on parole said he only went to AA meetings to get a needed paper signed saying he had attendance there.

Went to Blarney Stone bar where I felt uncomfortable just drinking club soda. An attorney drinking vodka asked me if Lauren and I are back together. When my response was negative he said, "Be careful who you get mixed up with on a rebound. Men in America are sitting ducks for hundreds of angry AIDS-infected women—some hell-bent on revenge on guys before they die. These dying women are among the most dangerous serial killers. I've talked to a guy who has talked to hundreds of women whose dreams of a happy and full life have been destroyed because of some guy. One night stands and with some jerk they met in a bar. Women who can really turn guys on. All kinds of women are angry, hurt and want to infect any guy who'll go to bed with them. They show no remorse, no guilt..."

"What about hundreds of guys whose dreams of a happy and full life have been destroyed because of some women?" I asked. "You want balanced objectivity, OK they're as bad. When has there been a time when we've had so many serial killers?"

When the attorney left, a girl called Dianne got on my nerves kidding me about my skinny arms (not in any mood for teasing). Someone else annoyed me with his suggestions as to what I should do about Lauren. On the way to my room, had mind transference contact with Lauren asking if I could go to apartment tomorrow evening. She said OK.

October 8, 1993   Diary to Lauren Morgan

Cough is persistent. Thinking about probation and letter and counseling. Went to apartment in the evening where Lauren made cheese and mushroom toast. She's a very good cook when she wants to be. Later, she had some rum and beer, getting tacky.

October 9, 1993   Diary to Lauren Morgan

Lauren fed cats and went to discount store for groceries and to the liquor store, returning close to noon. She had obviously been drinking and said when LeMay stayed there recently, he got annoyed saying some of my belongings were still in dresser drawers and closets of the room he used and he would like my stuff out of the apartment. She said she tried to explain to LeMay that I had moved to a small room which didn't seem to be large enough to hold all my stuff. LeMay said my stuff in the apartment could be put in some storage space he had elsewhere. I told Lauren I didn't want any of his storage space and that I would find a place of my own for my stuff. This puts pressure on me to get the rest of my stuff out of the apartment. To get belongings of mine had been some of my excuses for going to the apartment. What better excuse will I have to continue going to the apartment? One excuse used to be to watch TV. Now, Lauren has said I could have the extra TV that's used in the kitchen. She took a nap from 12 to 3pm. My cough is annoying. Feel tired. When Lauren got up, she said she was thinking about how I didn't keep my promise about taking care of her.

October 11, 1993   Diary to Lauren Morgan

Up early, fed cats, had coffee and packed bags to go. Lauren said before I left that I'm only nice and affectionate when I'm leaving the apartment. "Because I'm going and miss being with you," I told her. She looked great last Friday with grey checked dress and red belt and scarf. She still very much has what it takes when she gets her act together. Had lunch at Blarney Stone. Met a guy there who wants to sell a small refrigerator for $25. Said I'd take it. Felt tired in the evening and in my small room alone, felt depressed.

October 13, 1993   Diary to Lauren Morgan

Boss paid me off the books yesterday. I told him I'd have to go to Bellevue Hospital if my cough doesn't get better. Feel a little short of breath today. Having trouble breathing. Had to rest. Got to walk-in clinic at hospital today before 9 am. The doctor gave me antibiotics and alupent breath inhaler prescription. Was given a referral slip to 29th Street and 1st Avenue. Returned to work around 3pm. Took vitamin pills. After work, I had problem getting up the stairs to my room.

October 15, 1993   Diary to Lauren Morgan

One of the girls left the company in the middle of the afternoon over some personality clash in the office. A fellow at the office said the boss will put me on the payroll in a few weeks.

Chapter Forty Five

As previously arranged for a weekend trip to Atlantic City, LeMay met Lauren outside her apartment building in a convertible Cadillac. The weather was pleasant as they made their way through the Lincoln Tunnel to the New Jersey Turnpike and to exit 11, on to the Garden State Parkway, then the Atlantic City Expressway and to the heart of Atlantic City—a 130-mile trip taking about two and a half hours.

After parking, they made their way to the Boardwalk and stopped in at almost all the major casinos—Resorts International, Sands, Claridge, Bally's Park Place, Caesar's Atlantic City, Trump Plaza, Elsinore's Atlantis, Tropicana and Golden Nugget—some of which are a town unto itself with almost endless rows of slot machines and table after table of roulette, black jack and crapps. LeMay bet heavily after giving Lauren $1000 to bet as she pleased. LeMay played squares 1-18 and 19-36 every four times, having a winning streak with this cycle. After being at a gaming table for a while, they would go to the Boardwalk for a breather while looking out at the mighty Atlantic.

A hotel that impressed Lauren was Trump Plaza, perhaps because she won $300 there at a roulette table. She wanted to use her camera which she had brought but this was prohibited where there was gambling. There were the mirrors, being one way. Security guards and closed circuit TV seemed everywhere.

Following this, they went to Trump's Castle, off the Boardwalk, on the other side of the town near Harrah's Marina, taking a jitney to get there.

Following more gaming and the dinner, they took in a night show called "An Evening at LaCage" at one of the cabarets, with all female impersonators said to be more like women than women are like themselves—superbly comical. Lauren laughed 'til tears came down her cheeks, seated at a reserved table right at the end of the runway—said by some to be the best table in the house. They also took in Caesar's Bacchanal restaurant with its impressive black and green marble, statues and fountains.

While they were eating, LeMay said he thought, from having visited Atlantic City previously, the nightly entertainment spots could do with more rap.

"For your artists?" Lauren asked.

"We could have a show with rap artists in strange if not weird outfits, some bare chested, with an entourage of scantily clad female dancers—turning a solo presentation into a floorshow, in common with a review. Comedy, and breakdancing too, thrown into the mix."

"Without any gangsta thing creeps in?"

"It was gangsta with a thug past in the first place that indicated they too could blend into rap."

"Wearing oversize clothing worn backwards?"

"Rather than sugarcoating their gangsta lyrics, they went wild the other way—extremists."

"With unclear mumbling in their lyrics."

"Unnecessary with, 'Elvis was a hero to most, but he doesn't mean s--- to me.'"

"In a rap show in Florida, a rapper flashed his lewd nakedness at the audience. Rather than being arrested, he was just told to tone it down."

"Sometimes," said LeMay, "a rapper will go into some kind of a strip tease to get more attention when rapping about the tough life in the ghetto, telling it the way they see it—street chronicles."

"One rapper boasted of being a pimp and bragged about his rough treatment of women."

"Low-down brand of rap."

"Words like 'whore' and 'bitch' all too common, even among some female rappers, seeming to dwell on degradation of women," Lauren said.

"Others balance this with self-respect and dignity."

"Some with a message that some women need more than a nice guy, some women using their sexuality as weapons or means of persuasion in a male-dominated world."

"The market got wide open, big and bold enough for songs about guns and murder—hip hop and rap based on breaking rules because there was a big money to be made doing it. Not just about money, life and women, not dressed only in black leather jackets but black jeans, white Nike sneakers and oversize gold chains that could be readily marketed not only to black kids but white kids."

"Sad."

Well into the night, LeMay and Lauren made their way to and retired in a suite at Resorts International, facing the Atlantic.

They awoke around mid-morning, took their time getting up, had brunch, got absorbed in more gambling and went for a swim. A siesta followed and they had dinner at Trump Plaza before driving back to New York City.

Chapter Forty Six

Mark experienced more shortness of breath, which he took alupent for. Having been sober 107 days, he was trying to think positively. He had a room of his own (even though too small) and was getting along with Lauren so he could have a chance of occasional weekend time with her, the cats and the apartment. Still, his knees were a problem and he felt a lack of strength, muscle and air. He felt he must get rid of what he thought could be bronchitis and start exercising to get in shape. He might be getting his job back to the status he experienced before he lost it.

October 19, 1993   Diary to Lauren Morgan

Have to take puff of alupent every few hours. Contacted Lauren to meet me at Blarney Stone after work. Can't breathe. Feeling depressed, thinking I'll most probably have to go to hospital. Breathing almost impossible. The thought and expectation of what could be in store makes me furious. Lauren met me at Blarney Stone and as I felt terrible, she got a taxi and took me to Bellevue Emergency Ward. She stayed for five minutes. I told her to go. Nurse took me to Asthma emergency and put me on breathing vapor machine.

October 20, 1993   Diary to Lauren Morgan

In hospital. Met another fellow with same thing as I, Tim Hamilton, from Feltham, London, who sold houses in San Francisco and had had an interest in a TV production company. Very religious, prays in bed and at foot on knees and talks to himself. Treated well in hospital. Nurses and others attentive. Food good.

October 21, 1993   Diary to Lauren Morgan

Discharged from hospital. Went into a thought transfer contact with Lauren who made it known she didn't want me to come to the apartment that night as I had requested. Said she was going out. Wouldn't tell me who with. She said I'm acting like everything is OK and it is not. Went to see my probation officer, a woman—pleasant. She also has asthma and has to take spray every day. Meeting worked out OK.

October 22, 1993   Diary to Lauren Morgan

Coughing up green phlegm. Picked up small second hand refrig. Lauren contacted me. Said she had things to do on the weekend so I couldn't come to the apartment. I revealed I was hoping to be able to spend part of the weekend in the apartment resting and taking pills. She overlooked what I was hoping for. What have I done with my life? Wasted years and have nothing.

October 23, 1993   Diary to Lauren Morgan

Went to see my son, living with his grandmother. She showed me a copy of a letter my wife had written in her younger days to the Birmingham News, which said,

"In each presidential election year, the subject of voting is revived as a controversial topic for discussion. In our democratic society, the right to vote is a basic tenet of our belief in the right of the individual to have a voice in the government. In recent times, some political philosophers have advanced the theory that the power to vote should rest with a more selective cross-section of the population, and proposed that prospective voters pass an intelligence test as a prerequisite to voting. It is claimed that this practice could result in election of more competent government officials than is now the case."

My mother-in-law was upset over the efforts of the finishing school for ladies not being able to change my wife back to the way she was before her heart transplant. My mother-in-law, extremely fond of my son, is doing a terrific job bringing him up—well-mannered, polite, considerate—the kind of son you dream of having. No heart donor available for the boy yet. Waiting. Calling on a higher power in me to help me help my son, who's more deserving of living than I. When I got back to my small room, I listened to the radio—nostalgic show; Ink Spots, Andrew Sisters, Russ Columbo's "When The Blue Of The Night." He paved the way for Bing Crosby. Lonely. Having breathing trouble and coughing. Miss apartment, Lauren and the cats.

Chapter Forty Seven

Mark woke up from a nightmare about noises and women's spirits in his room. After telling Beth about it, she went into his room and dispelled the spirits with, "Jesus commands you to leave (pause and then loudly) NOW."

October 25, 1993   Diary to Lauren Morgan

Feel congestion in the front part of my chest. Listened to Chicago Symphony for a couple of hours—Tchaikovsky violin concert and symphony #4. Got to thinking of this terrible year—jail, three-year probation sentence, no room of my own to stay in for too long, in hospital, Lauren meeting LeMay.

October 26, 1993   Diary to Lauren Morgan

Blue Monday yesterday, following a blue weekend. Unsure of what to do. Very cautious so I won't be disappointed and angry with myself for rushing into something too fast. Have no idea what I want to do with my time other than working and being paid off the books. This morning at work, Lauren contacted me. I asked if OK to come to apartment. She said OK. When I arrived in the evening, she looked rested. Said LeMay took her to Atlantic City over a recent weekend. I asked her if she loves him. She said, "Possibly not, but he's helpful."

"As I suppose you are to him," I said. She added, "It's no free lunch for either of us." She said I could stay the night to get more of my belongings from the apartment together to take back with me in the morning. She added I could have her kitchen TV set. (Another little push—leaving me less reason to come to the apartment.) Felt lonely as I set to packing more of my belongings, wondering into the night what there is for me to look forward to.

Chapter Forty Eight

Mark was up early, did some more packing, fed the cats, had coffee and left the apartment with more of his belongings which he took to his small room before going to the office. He was worried about his hospital bill and would try to get Medic Aid assistance.

October 29, 1993   Diary to Lauren Morgan

Lauren contacted me at work. Said I could come to apartment for TV set and more of my belongings. Went there after work. She made a very nice dinner for us. Then while I was doing more packing, she was on the phone for over an hour and said after that she had to go out, hinting she didn't want me in the apartment when she wasn't there. When I said half spiteful and half kidding, "I'll stay the night," she said, "Oh no you won't." The message, she doesn't want me there any more other than to pick up my belongings, really hurt. She also said that at one time when I had been intolerable with drinking, she had wished I was dead. Her mood swings amaze me. I packed a suitcase with shirts, personal papers, note pads, socks, black corduroy pants, black and red jacket and other

156

clothes. Took these and TV set Lauren offered me from her apartment to my room. Depressed, as situation much more pronounced and serious now with LeMay more in the picture. Likely future separation from her and apartment and cats and comfortable temporary routine existence I have known there. Went to the Blarney Stone where I met the attorney who knew about my wife's condition and my mother-in-law's suggestion that Sandra attend courses at a finishing school. "Had her attendance at the finishing school been helpful?" he asked. "It hadn't worked out as had been hoped." Going to my room, I felt my mind not completely alert. Drink a lot of coffee while smoking. Must try to pull out of this depression. I miss her terribly. Doubt if my pride can ever forgive her and myself for what she has done to me.

November 2, 1993   Diary to Lauren Morgan

Depressed mental state is affecting me physically. Feeling some chest congestion. Went to hospital to see about bill I owe them. Showed them documents I had brought and signed application for Medic Aid. They said I would hear from them in two months about whether they pay all or part of my hospital bill. Killed time in the afternoon at work. Very depressed in the evening in small room alone, thinking and brooding over Lauren. Chain coffee-drinking along with chain smoking. Torturing myself with nasty vindictive verbal revenge thoughts and thoughts of more than verbal revenge. I have a .38 caliber hand gun with silencer that I bought when Juan said he was going to come back to this building and shoot me if I told the truth about him at trial. I can't go on like this.

November 3, 1993   Diary to Lauren Morgan

Feel congestion in chest and coughing up phlegm. Am using different medication. Congestion building. It's an effort to breathe deeply when lying down. Feel a little weaker each day. Feeling short of breath. Short of air. Slightest exertion leaves me short of breath. Coughing up green phlegm. Depression bad, with asthma, Lauren situation, room too small, my son… Wonder how long I can last…

November 4, 1993   Diary to Lauren Morgan

Breathing OK when I'm still. Drink coffee and rest. Don't want to exert myself. Ask Jesus to help me, per Beth's suggestion. I hear her saying sometimes to herself, "God help me. God help me." Thinking about Lauren again. Wise thing to do is not be mean and nasty, which is what I want to do—cause her pain and make her feel bad. Bronchitis back again. I don't think it was ever completely knocked out. Think breathing machine at hospital might knock off asthma, at least for a while. Drink almost a dozen cups of coffee a day. Feeling temporarily comfortable sitting by window against pillow. Nagging depression won't leave me over Lauren and health.

November 5, 1993   Diary to Lauren Morgan

Coughing up more phlegm. Can't lie down. Had dream and can't remember it. Took different medications and vitamins with coffee. Contacted Lauren and told her I'm going to the hospital. She said, "I'll talk to you on Monday." Had more coffee and contacted Lauren again for spite and told her, "You're glad I'm out of the way for the weekend so you can let that guy do anything he wants with you." She got annoyed and said, "Don't talk to me like that or I'll cut you off." She drifted off to lost contact. I realize this does no good, but the nagging depression over her has me doing it. I have to watch the probation angle. She could maybe say I'm harassing her. Listening to Rackmanenoff's 3rd Piano Concerto, reading New York News, smoking and drinking coffee and trying to talk to myself out of going to the hospital. Trouble breathing when I move. Find myself scheming over what to do to Lauren because of the nagging depression over her (that I'm also responsible for). Can understand reports I hear and read about of guys doing away with their better halves and themselves. I can identify with that. Scheming revenge, bits and pieces while listening to classical music. The composers of music with deep feeling must have felt what I feel.

Chapter Forty Nine

Mark was having trouble breathing. Coughing up yellow phlegm, he felt hospital might be necessary. In trying to take a nap, he had a weird dream he couldn't get together. With almost no breath, he took alupent over ten minutes in preparation to go to the Emergency Ward at the hospital. He walked down the stairs, resting at every landing, and got a taxi to Bellevue. He was taken to the Asthma room and put on the vapor machine right away.

November 7, 1993   Diary to Lauren Morgan

All night on vapor machine. Thinking bad thoughts about Lauren. Must get out of the hospital. Nurses all very nice and professional. One of the girls said next time I should go to the Veterans Hospital on 23rd Street where they would take me in right away and treat me like a king.

November 8, 1993   Diary to Lauren Morgan

Given prescriptions and discharged from hospital in the afternoon. Contacted Lauren and asked to go to apartment. She said to meet her at the Blarney Stone. Met her there at 5pm. We sat at a table and talked. She told me she didn't want me in the apartment any more except to remove the last of my belongings and see the cats, who have lost some of the fondness they used to have for me. After she left, depression moved in like ocean waves moving shoreward.

Went to my room, slumped on the cot and fell asleep. Awoke a couple of hours later, got out my .38 caliber hand gun with silencer, practiced aiming it, put it in a shoulder strap I had bought and put that on. Torment awful. I mind-communicated with Lauren. She revealed she was in the bar across the street from her apartment with LeMay. I left my small room for that area, looked through the window of the bar across from her building. She was there with LeMay, drinking and laughing. I looked on in agony. I moved to a window in the shadow at the side of the building, pointed my .38 at them. My heart was pounding, blood rushing to my head. All I had to do was press my forefinger twice and each of them would be dead. I held that at-the-ready-position. A flash flared in me—my son. What about my son—his need for a heart donor? If I shot them and myself there, how would it be known I wanted my heart donated to him. I had to think about it. I wanted my heart donated to him. I wanted my heart donated to my son if no other donor's heart was forthcoming. I walked away. Nothing was done. I returned to my small room.

Chapter Fifty

Mark's wife, Sandra, who was living with her sister in New Jersey, was out jogging on the outskirts of Jersey City, when she saw a young, well-conditioned girl jogging a short distance ahead of her. Sandra jogged up to even with her saying, "Hi. Been jogging long?"

"Since getting into boxing," the other girl replied.

"As a boxer?"

"Yes."

"What's your name?" Sandra asked.

"Rina Tarler. At first, I just went to the gym for exercise—a change from sitting at a computer. Since it was a boxing gym, I got to doing boxing exercise."

"Which gym?"

"Like to see it?"

"Yes."

The two jogged on to Sheldon's Gym where male and female boxers were working out. In the gym, Rina got to talking to Sam Sheldon, a small, thin man with scars that told you he had been a long time fighter. Rina introduced Sandra to Sam, adding that he was a trainer.

"A licensed trainer and coach," Sam added and asked Sandra, "Done any boxing?"

"No."

"Look around the place. You see a few doing exercises, some punching the little fast bag, some the big bag, some shadow boxing, some sparring..."

"Interesting."

"Get involved if you want. Suggest you just start with exercising, touching your toes with your hands, jumping while you spread your arms, pushups..."

Sandra went through exercises Sam suggested. Before leaving, she asked Rina, "When is the next session?"

"The place is open every day except Sunday."

"I'll be back," Sandra said.

Chapter Fifty One

November 11, 1993   Diary to Lauren Morgan

Lauren contacted me at the office. Said she had a couple of letters addressed to me at the apartment. Arranged to meet her at the Blarney Stone after her work. Somebody at the office said he heard the boss saying he'll put me on regular payroll shortly. Met Lauren at Blarney Stone after work. She gave me my mail and said LeMay wouldn't be at the apartment and asked if I'd like to go to apartment to pick up some of my belongings. Said OK. Apartment not very clean. Had some sausage and eggs there—good. We got along OK, but no romance or affection. She said LeMay would feed the cats while she's away on Christmas week, meaning, there wouldn't be a need for me to be in the apartment on Christmas week. At least, she gave me a good meal before that salvo. I collected some of my belongings and returned to my room. Felt sad. Seem lost. All night thinking of Lauren and LeMay. Nothing in sight to be with her for weekend in foreseeable future, except to pick up some more of my stuff. Listened to Tchaikovsky's Symphony #4.

November 13, 1993   Diary to Lauren Morgan

Browsed over some of my nonsensical papers I had brought back from the apartment, which at least temporarily took my mind off my depression. Went to see my son in the afternoon.

November 18, 1993   Diary to Lauren Morgan

Stomach queasy. Skipped breakfast. Feel tired. Coughing, congestion phlegm, some shortage of breath. At work, boss called me aside and said he wants to put me on more responsible work. Had temporary illusion maybe someday, I can have a house again, a shelter against the future, get all my things in one place again in a place big enough to hold them, have a studio for painting, collages, art and metal pieces on boards and my own place to study. Saw probation officer— mostly talk about asthma we both have. Don't have to see her again for a couple of months. Lauren contacted me to say some mail came for me to apartment. She met me at the Blarney Stone after work. She had rum and beer; I, BBQ chicken. Said she had period pains. No emotion at all. She said I could visit the cats for two hours next week, at which time I can pick up more of my belongings. LeMay has been asking her when all of my stuff is going to be out of the apartment and if, instead of my picking up a few things at a time, I couldn't have a truck or van drive up and clear all of the rest of my stuff out; which would mean I'd have no logical reason to go to the apartment anymore. Very depressed.

November 21, 1993   Diary to Lauren Morgan

Some congestion and coughing, stomach queasy, some shortage of breath. Took alupine and prednisone. Have tightness in chest. Very depressed over Lauren and worsening health because of her. Have to go to hospital again—this time to Veterans Hospital. Took cab there. They gave me prescriptions.

November 22, 1993   Diary to Lauren Morgan

Released from hospital. At work today, boss paid me off the books. In the evening, found I had to expand my lungs to get air. Taking so many prescriptions I don't know how it will all mix! What if I should die in my sleep without people knowing my heart is to be donated to my son. I will sleep with a note pinned at the front of me that if I die my heart is to be immediately donated to my son.

November 25, 1993   Diary to Lauren Morgan

In a.m. this Thanksgiving, listened to Mozart Requiem. In part of the afternoon, I listened to Rachmaninoff Piano Concerto #2, Afternoon Of A Faun. Lonely, thinking of Lauren. Chest congestion and green phlegm. Have chest cold or bronchitis. Feel weaker each day. If I don't put my revenge thoughts into action, I could find myself grown too weak to carry them out. I will try to focus. Lonely and depressed, more hate for Lauren and LeMay. Moping and brooding very unhealthy mentally and physically. Feel ball of congestion in middle chest. Apprehensive about my physical condition and if it will clear up without taking pills and spray all the time. Went to chest clinic and obtained prescription before going to work.

Was feeling depressed coming home from work when I met Beth in the hall who said she had run into Lauren on Madison Avenue near 37th Street. I followed Beth to her room where she put on some water for coffee for us and pointed to the chair on the other side of her table which I seated myself on. Beth added that when she bumped into Lauren, she invited her to the apartment. When she got there, Lauren told her she and LeMay had done some all-night night-clubbing, going from one place to another, getting real high in which (Lauren) let her mouth run about LeMay possibly being on drugs and possibly having some connection with the Mafia, and that LeMay had warned her to stop. Lauren added that LeMay had put it to her in a manner of a threat.

November 26, 1993   Diary to Lauren Morgan

Lauren contacted me with a mental telepathy message at the office to say there was no mail for me at apartment, which struck me as strange because the only time she contacted me before about mail at the apartment was when there was mail there to be forwarded to me. She went on to reveal she had a cold or something and was taking antibiotics. She didn't say anything about wanting more of my belongings taken out of the apartment. I got the impression she communicated in the manner of her wanting me to mentally hold her hand for a few minutes. She didn't say anything about LeMay.

Chapter Fifty Two

On the weekend of November 27 & 28, LeMay took Lauren to a getaway out of the country—Acapulco on the Mexican Riviera, a nice laid-back contrast to the big city's glitz. They booked in at Las Brisas, an unusual resort high on a hillside overlooking Acapulco Bay. Where hallways are roads, elevators are jeeps and rooms are a village of 300 casitas with a private or shared swimming pool (theirs being a private pool), a stocked refrigerator, bar, lighted tennis courts, gold, skin diving, water skiing and sailing.

They enjoyed a scotch and soda, which LeMay had prepared from their bar, while looking at the outlying scenery—green foothills and mountains descending gracefully to beautiful blue bay and ocean waters—the turquoise water of the bay area setting off this resort city's string of high rise hotels. They were at what was said to be the most famous of Mexico's seaside resorts where the temperature during the year got hardly warmer than 91 degrees nor colder than 72.

"Yawning," LeMay asked, "because of me or are you tired?"

"I could do with a nap but this place is too nice to waste on sleep."

"Let's get out and around then."

They made their way to and into a decorated horse-drawn carriage which passed along Costera Miguel Ademan. The driver informed them that Acapulco was once the main west coast seaport for the Manila galleons and their treasures from the Orient. From here, silks, spices and other exotic goods were carried overland on mules to Mexico City and Veracruz for shipment to Spain. The rich trade with the Orient attracted English pirates, among others, Sir Francis Drake being one of them. As time passed Acapulco lapsed into lethargy of an almost forgotten fishing village and then to what is said to be one of the top resorts of Mexico's most popular partying spots.

"We'll do our part to uphold this reputation," LeMay added.

He and Lauren visited shops, for those who like to dress in typical resort fashion, which stocked designers' dresses, blouses, shirts, sports clothes and more including silk panties in sets of 7 with each pair having the day of the week sewn in, which LeMay insisted on buying for Lauren.

They returned to their hotel, swam in their outdoor pool clad in little more than suntan oil and while drying themselves in the sun, LeMay commented, "I'm wondering how we can work rap in down here."

"Diluting their culture with rap?"

"It's already a much-diluted culture. What comes to mind is letting artists dragged in by hip hop drag in others down here, mixing in break dancing and female dancers with as little on as can be gotten away with."

"And considering what you can find down here that you can take back to New York?"

"Of course. What we brought down here wouldn't have to be about glorifying killing somebody; nor would it have to be about who has more guns or more kilos."

"Like what?"

"Could be about what these people down here see around them."

"Like tourists with their other language out to enjoy, within their means, the best of what they have to offer?"

"I was thinking more along the lines of rapping about what they find in checking up on their roots and culture."

"Hoping they won't get so charged up, they become violent with words that'll evolve into being acted out for real?"

"We'd hope it wouldn't be hip hop based on crushing your enemy-ego getting out of control."

"In keeping it real, but no so real it'll cost you your life, where do you draw the line?"

"The old-timers had it under control. Listen to them and update, hopefully without violence, but if there is a demand for it, it's the way the chips fall."

"You talk like the Mafia sometimes."

"Don't let me hear you say that again. And don't ever say that to another –that I talk like the Mafia. No talk about me that way.

This guy could be ruthless, Lauren thought; but he was very generous. They got dressed and following a meal at a nearby restaurant, had a siesta which was short.

As they were dressing again, LeMay suggested she put on a pair of the set of silk panties he had bought her for each day in the week. As she was doing so he added, "They could sell lot of those if they had printed on each pair, instead of the day of the week, the day of the week with a.m. and on another pair the same day of the week with p.m., suggesting a week's supply set of 14 instead of 7."

"Hadn't thought of you as a marketing consultant for ladies silk panties."

"Keep on not thinking it."

After dressing they gallivanted to some of the 9-mile stretch of glittering hotels and nightspots along the bay shore, indulging in Acapulco's reputation for wild night life—music, tangos, flamenco dancing, standup comedy on into the morning hours to almost sunrise—including watching diving from LaQuebrada cliff, where from a torch-lit spot atop a natural rock, men from mid-teens to mid-forties dove from a hundred and thirty five feet, the success of their spectacular diving depending not only on skill but split second timing, since the tide filled the swirling surf and then receded quickly.

Wearily, they made their way back to their hotel to go about the same ritual they had gone through at Saratoga and Atlantic City.

He said to her while she looked to his face, "Know what's going through my mind?"

"Haven't any idea."

"Rap lyrics about the sex drive being second only to hunger."

"Could be worked on."

"By a successful rapper, maybe, who might have an entourage of a dozen hangers on. Money of some goes into stocks and bonds they think will go up forever. One guy rapped about stock market—how he sold before the crash of '87 and bought in when it started to go up again."

"I guess rap isn't just a momentary fad after all."

"You can be on top one moment—living and traveling top style, staying in the swankiest suites and going to the best clubs and then, fall to living in a squalid one room with no phone and no furniture, then living from cardboard box to cardboard box, after being a short time darling of the rap industry."

"Hope the sun doesn't set on your kingdom."

"That's better. Where was I?"

"Hoping you don't have a big fall."

"One rapper said he had dealt with politicians and he had dealt with gangsters and he found gangsters to be more honorable. Oh-h-h-h-...."

"What is it?"

"A stomach pain. It's OK. Look at me so we look into each other's eyes and into each other's souls. Oh-h-h-h…"

"Oh-oh. Stomach pains—worse than I thought." He got up, went to his suit coat and went into the bathroom with it. In the bathroom he took a package of opium from the pocket and gave himself 35 grains.

Stomach pain, which had been occurring for the past few years, had driven him to taking opium for relief. Time in between seeing Lauren and others, he had preferred to be by himself. Taking opium had seemed to be phenomenal to him as his pain ceased and he knew boundless pleasure. There was no intoxication as from wine or spirits—only a sense of being utterly at peace with the world and himself. It uplifted his spirit and when its effect wore off, there wasn't much depression. Some of his greatest pleasure had been that of withdrawing himself at a time when the opium had reached its maximum effect on his mind so that he could get the most enjoyment from his opium-induced visions and dreams. He had spells of wanting to withdraw from this and be with Lauren. He liked the way her body was shaped and how it felt. Although he had been taking opium about once a week, he felt he had not become a slave to the drug. He found himself able to reduce the amount taken with longer intervals between the doses.

When LeMay returned to Lauren from the bathroom, she was awake with concern. He told her he was OK. He added he wanted peace and quiet and dozed off to sleep.

While lying there, Lauren found herself into mind transfer communication with Mark. "I just wanted to say, hello," she said.

"Where are you? Are you OK?" Mark asked.

"Yes," Lauren answered and contact faded off.

Part of the beauty of the morning was missed with LeMay and Lauren sleeping in until mid-morning. After brunch, they took a yacht cruise in the bay area and then went swimming about seven miles north of Acapulco at Pie dela Cuesta where a deserted beach offered a nice laid-back sense of peace. From there, they made their way to a spot where they both went parasailing—from a standing position, a speedboat hauling them in parasailing gear so they rose to an altitude of some 300 feet flying around the surrounding area over the water.

They ate at a thatched café—an almost perfect place to watch a sunset turn to Pacific into gold.

Lauren felt, with mixed emotions, she was getting somewhat spoiled as they made their way back to their hotel and got ready for their flight back to New York.

Chapter Fifty Three

Mark was thinking about belongings of his still to be moved from the apartment to his small room. It seemed it could come to a point where there'd be but enough space left for him to ease himself in and out of his room, if he turned himself sideways.

December 3, 1993   Diary to Lauren Morgan

I'm reminded of a guy on this same top floor where I live who has a small room and met a girl who broke up with her husband and asked this short guy to store her belongings in his small room, which he has done. But in doing so, finds there's no space left in his room for him; so he now sleeps outside of his room in front of the door. Came dangerously close to going into a liquor store and buying a bottle of cognac. Grand architect of the universe guide me. Have fantasy of winning at LOTTO or big in the stock market. Shortage of breath not good.

December 6, 1993   Diary to Lauren Morgan

Contacted Lauren to go up to apartment in the evening. She said OK. Took subway up after work. Greeted cats. Drank coffee while moving hardcover books to right side of the room I used to occupy there. She took back two Maugham books and Vanity Fair. I told her I was depressed about confinement in small room away from the apartment, cats, and her. Collected a lot of personal stuff to go from apartment to my small room. While she was taking a shower, I noticed in her bedroom drawer some of LeMay's socks and underwear, which I took out of there and threw on the living room floor. After that, I put two handfuls of Ajax cleanser powder into her best plant. Then I got so full of remorse and guilt, I had to admit it to Lauren and helped her clean it out. Told her I didn't know why I did it except for hate revenge. She forgave me before I left. On the way back to my small room, I got to thinking that what I did to her plant could impede future efforts to come back to the apartment. What if she got to thinking I might put Ajax in her food next time? Back in my small room, I unpacked from suitcases things I had brought from apartment. Feel increasing depression and loneliness again. Can't get rid of bronchitis in my chest.

Chapter Fifty Four

Someone at Mark's office told Mark his boss was asking about him (Mark). He didn't elaborate, causing Mark to wonder if it was about him continuing on the wagon or something else. After work, Mark went through personal papers, which didn't relieve his brooding over Lauren.

December 9, 1993   Diary to Lauren Morgan

Feel tightness in my chest. Lauren communicated with me in latter part of the afternoon. Says she wants to talk—sounds like she doesn't want the suspense of when and how long I'll be coming to the apartment. Wondering if I could get a job outside of firm I'm with—reputation being not so good because of drink. Country doing well but too much of it is not. Not enough sharing. As Shakespeare said, "They're as sick that surfeit with too much as those that suffer with naught."

December 12, 1993   Diary to Lauren Morgan

Lauren contacted me at office on Friday. Said OK to come to apartment Sunday for a couple of hours. Wants me to communicate with her first on Sunday.

Today, Sunday, communicated with Lauren and went to apartment. Nice to see the cats. Stroked and patted their smooth fur. Lauren said while I got to sorting out more of my stuff, that she was going out to do some shopping. Lonely and depressed being there alone going through my stuff. Drank a lot of coffee. Lauren returned a couple of hours later bombed.

She cooked fish fillets, mashed potatoes, cheese and spinach—very good. After the meal, she continued sipping rum and beer and then went into her room and slept; in fact she slept the rest of the day, having forgotten she had said I was to be there for two hours in the morning. I went to the bed I used to sleep in there, laid down and dozed off with the two cats.

December 13, 1993   Diary to Lauren Morgan

Up early, fed cats, had coffee, got my stuff together to take from the apartment. She disputed over who owned some of the things and threatened not to let me come back. She took a shower as I was leaving. I still have feelings for her. At work, asked if I could go on payroll soon. They didn't seem to know. Contacted Lauren and asked if she wanted to have lunch with me. Said she didn't feel good but would meet after work sometime this week and explain why it's over if I wanted her to. After work, went to AA meeting. All through it was thinking of Lauren. Would be better if I could think of her as not being part of me.

December 20, 1993   Diary to Lauren Morgan

Went to Bellevue Hospital on Friday and got prescriptions. Annoyed and lonely. Play LOTTO. Once, I got five numbers right and received only about $1,000. Don't spread the money out evenly. Contacted Lauren today. She doesn't want me at the apartment like family. Angry and depressed with her mood swings. Feel breathing problem coming on. Went to work from 1pm to 5pm. Brood all the time over Lauren and apartment and cats. Depression level varies but always present.

Chapter Fifty Five

Mark' wife, Sandra, went to Sheldon' boxing gym again. While going through boxing exercises, Rina came in and joined her. After doing exercise, Sandra watched Rina punch the small fast punching bag with uncanny speed—the bag going from side to side and front and back with Rina sometimes using only one hand. Sandra tried it, with less awesome results. Rina then punched the big bag, which Sandra also tried. Then Rina got into shadow boxing, with Sandra trying to imitate her.

While undressing after working up a sweat, to take a shower, Rina said to Sandra, "Boxing was used in ancient Greece to train youths to become warriors. Hundreds of years later there is boxing in England and France. In the early 1700s a guy called Figg opened a boxing school in London teaching gloveless, bare-knuckled fighting."

"When did the boxers start wearing gloves," Sandra asked.

"In the late 1800s the Marquess of Queensbury sponsored a code requiring boxers to wear gloves. Around the time, English boxers came to the U.S. trying to create interest in boxing. In 1920 New York passed a law allowing public prize-fighting. Boxing grew

"How about women boxers?" Sandra asked.

"They have recently become contestants in the sport. The National Women's Boxing Federation has been formed. I'm really excited about it."

"What took them so long to get women started? Sandra asked.

"A good question. The women who come here are serious about training. They originally focused on conditioning and got caught up in the sport—sparring and then completing."

"Some say women's boxing is a fad."

"My comment to that is women are dedicated. They train with a professional attitude, taking their frustrations out in this form. It can be grueling, but let me add, women in boxing are here to stay."

Chapter Fifty Six

December 21, 1993   Diary to Lauren Morgan

Coughed up big gobs green phlegm—have bronchitis again. Told a guy in the office I wouldn't mind a hot scotch and a lemon drink for my bronchitis. Boss heard and threatened me: "If you come in soused you're out." After climbing five flights of stairs when I got home, I had breathing problem.

December 22, 1993   Diary to Lauren Morgan

Lauren contacted me at the office in the afternoon. Met her after work at the Blarney Stone. She said LeMay wants to put what stuff I have left in the apartment in the storage and doesn't want me to come to apartment after my stuff is put in storage. She first sweetened this veiled threat with an offer to have a medical prescription refilled for me. I told her I seemed to be running into a problem trying to get all my belongings into my small room. She said some of my belongings could be put in outer storage space that LeMay had. "Please work on it," she said while she paid for the drink I thought I had bought her and left.

December 23, 1993   Diary to Lauren Morgan

In the middle of afternoon, Lauren contacted me at office and said she got a prescription filled for me and would drop it off at the Blarney Stone. Told her I was depressed and coughing and was leaving work and would wait for her. Very close to drinking. Lauren met me at Blarney Stone and gave me filled prescription. I realize, in case any confirmation is needed, I still love her. She asked me what I would be giving my son for Christmas. It was with a sense of shame I realized I did not know. I said, "I must see my son, living with his mother's mother and of course, with a present for each." Lauren said of the many presents LeMay had given her she had a new wool scarf and silk blouse which I could give to my son and his grandmother as presents from me. I was very touched at her thoughtfulness. She had me go to her apartment with her where she wrapped the scarf and blouse in Christmas wrapping paper and affixed Christmas seals and tags. I didn't know how to thank her as she opened the door for me to leave the apartment. Depression started rolling in. Had thoughts later of contacting Lauren to tell her I need her and love her and can't stand the depression. In my small room, I watched Christmas shows which did nothing to decrease my depression.

December 24, 1993   Diary to Lauren Morgan

Feeling very low. Went to Blarney Stone. Felt too miserable to wish anyone a Merry Christmas. Thinking about contacting Lauren as memories come to mind of her and me in former Christmas seasons.

Contacted Lauren about 5:30, told her I wanted us to be together again. She said she didn't think it possible and went into an explanation that LeMay will stay there tonight and drive her to the airport in the morning. I asked her if she loved him. She said he's generous with her. I asked her to think about us and said I still love her. Asked her to call me when she comes back from spending Christmas with her father and relatives. Drank coffee and smoked in my small room as I watched TV. Started to see "A Christmas Carol" but too depressed to watch through all of it.

December 25, 1993   Diary to Lauren Morgan

Christmas day. Went to my son and his grandmother with presents for each. I had a very good Christmas dinner with them and from them I received, as well as Christmas dinner, a present of a comb and a chocolate bar. I felt the higher power in me I had called upon to make it through this day was helping me. I told the boy and his grandmother I was thinking of the woman I married, his mother and her daughter, who had thought she couldn't have children and had with me, before birth of our son, adopted a baby girl, seven months old, after the regular hassling with the community health offices, to see if we were fit parents. The usual bureaucratic nonsense. But we got her. But she was only with us a short time. We named her Ann Marie, Ann after my mother and Marie after hers. We had three cats and they thought Ann Marie was another cat when we put her on the floor. She was active and loved all the cats with almost equal affection, but she had her special favorite. She was curious and inquisitive about everything.

Shortly we noticed that she became tired very easily. She ate very little and had to sleep with that special cat who always had his paw on her arm. The loving touch was always there.

We took her to a parade of hospitals and specialists. She had some blood disease, a form of hemophilia that they couldn't cure. At school, she was smart. Little accolades were brought home regularly with beams in her eyes for kisses that she knew would be forthcoming.

And she would sit on my lap after dinner to watch an hour of TV before she got too sleepy. She brushed her teeth and kissed us both and said, "Goodnight mommy and daddy, I love you."

She would look at us with expectant, excited eyes that would melt any animosity we had against the world. Her little fingers that find your cheek would dispel all hatreds and depressions that build up during the work day.

She would talk to our cats, plants and flowers, and called them all by names she invented. She put all the plants and flowers together because she thought they might be lonely and in some way, talk to each other.

Later on, when they died it seemed sad because it chartered her tragic destiny. But she always perked up when we bought her new ones to name.

At about six years of age, she started getting very short of breath, sometimes gasping for air. We had to take her out of school. Then she almost stopped talking completely because of the painful effort. And one night in the living room with my wife, she just looked at us with such sad, soulful eyes touched with sorrow that we sensed she was leaving us.

I took her in my arms, with slow tears coming down my face, with her breathing more halted, with my desperate pleas of, "Please God, be merciful." I kissed her. After another rasping breath she whispered, "I love you mommy and daddy." And with a heavenly smile on her little face her life slipped away.

After telling my son and his grandmother of Ann Marie, the grandmother played the piano and the three of us sang Christmas carols. I left in the evening with a heavy heart, but with uplifted spirit.

Chapter Fifty Seven

Mark's wife, Sandra, at Sheldon's boxing gym again, went through boxing exercises with Rina and punched the fast little and large punching bags followed by shadow boxing. Sam Sheldon, having noticed them, walked over and said, "With head and chest protective gear as well as the gloves on, let Sandra here try to take shots at you, Rina, with you just protecting yourself. OK?"

"Sure."

After putting on their boxing gear, Sam said to the two while they got into the ring, "Each go to a corner. We'll try it for a two-minute round. Remember only with Sandra trying to hit you, Rina, and you just protecting yourself. Get it?"

"Sure."

With a stop watch, Sam said, "OK, go."

The two women came to the center of the ring with Rina in a protective stance, and Sandra jabbing. Rina backed off, danced to the left and right and came in bobbing and weaving to back off again as Sandra tried to hit her.

When the two-minute session of the punching stances of one and the protective stances of the other was over, Sam said, "You were flat-footed, Sandra, while Rina was on her toes, dancing around you, weaving, bowing, in, out, from side to side, seeking where she could have picked her shots."

"I never realized," said Sandra," I was so good at missing."

"Because Rina is hard to hit—a good defensive fighter. She's so unmarked you wouldn't guess she's a boxer when she's out of here. Tell her, Rina, how you felt when you went into the ring for your first fight outside of here."

"Frankly, I was scared and excited and a whole lot of things were going on inside me."

"Tell her how you feel about being roped in—no pun intended."

"Besides the fear, it's fun and educational."

"A great place," said Sandra, "to question your gender, strength, power and how far you can push yourself."

Chapter Fifty Eight

December 26, 1993   Diary to Lauren Morgan

Painful sentimentality of Christmas season won't go away. Went to Al Anon meeting where I at least, had company other than my own. I became attracted to Lauren because of some hidden course of the stars, with such a hold on me, I can't say in Lauren's case, as I could in the case of my wife, "When it's over it's over. Time to move on." The revenge thoughts I've had against Lauren and myself I never had against my wife.

December 28, 1993   Diary to Lauren Morgan

Depression creeping back. Trouble breathing. Not contacting any of my brothers or their wives prevents my being inquired into with their merciless curiosity. "How are you now? Where are you living?" "In a small room, in which I'm just about relegated to coming into sideways." How could I cover up my agonizing? Putting on a half-smile in the face of adversity is for an actor, which I'm not.

December 29, 1993   Diary to Lauren Morgan

Two days, after this, to go to the final day of the worst year of my life. Guy I know died yesterday of heart attack. He probably willed it. Loneliness returning. If I don't have something to live for, I do have something to die for—my heart for my son. Wanted to go to Blarney Stone for lunch, but in my state of mind, people saying "Happy New Year" would have me miserably upsetting to all around me.

December 30, 1993   Diary to Lauren Morgan

Had dream about Lauren making me jealous. Unconscious rebelling against me? Walked over to Billy Budd's bar and looked in the window. Went to AA meeting. Told Cindy she looked ravishing. She didn't remember my name. At one time I could have been referred to as intelligent, smart and someone with class but in moving through the hazards and minefields of life, I've changed into something I can hardly bear to recognize. Went back and looked across the street at Billy Budd's. Bar seemed full. Came home. Don't seem to be able to do anything about my state of depression.

December 31, 1993   Diary to Lauren Morgan

Last day of cruel year. Tired. Depression bad. Can't take another year like this.

Now lying down, lost in loneliness and with not even the temporary escape of alcohol, I shut out the New Year's noise of revelry and go to bed listening to Mozart's Symphony #28.

Chapter Fifty Nine

January 1, 1994   Diary to Lauren Morgan

Made it to a new year. Coughing green phlegm. Vienna Philharmonic playing Strauss. Must struggle for New Year's resolution. I will have on agenda effort to do writing, in addition to my diary. Make effort to get something published. Think of and review ideas for ads and promotions. A New Year burst of enthusiasm might improve my lot. Need more than burst, but step in right direction. End of old nightmare, beginning of new. New nightmare year?

Beth, in room next to mine, wished me a Happy New Year. Wished her same. Told her struggling to make New Year's resolution. She invited me to have coffee at small table in her room by open door. I owe her. Told her trying to get out of rut in New Year—review ideas for writing and ideas for ads and product promotions. Trying to enlarge on burst of enthusiasm. Said she was glad for me and would help if she could. Said I would like to try shot of scotch in coffee but dare not. She said she would not either so, as not to feel she's having something I'm not having. To someone that doesn't know Beth, she seems laid back, as if she had hardly a care. What she seems and what she is are different. She has been frightened and hurt, which she tries to keep to herself. In knowing Beth, I realize how much more an older woman has to offer than a young one. She has known heartbreak, she's understanding and motherly—a human being you find it easy to become fond of.

Am trying to get involved in writing—something I have lived or know of. Beth says when you find something you feel you can't take time from to eat or sleep, you have found what you want to do. She said she used to go around talking to herself saying, "God help me. Dear God help me. Oh God I'm not running right. Please Jesus, help me. She said in those days, she would sit tense and not lean back in a chair with ease and every little while, put her fingers to her mouth and bite her fingernails. She, like I, would feel she wanted to get something done and feel something was holding her back. She knew she would be taking her vitamin pills, but let that go. When a girl friend of hers suggested back then that she visit a public psychologist, Beth says she didn't answer. She let things slide and got run down. Didn't keep hospital appointments. Got to lacking an interest in living and seemed content to letting herself run down to nothing. With the coaxing of her girlfriend, Beth did go to see a public psychologist. She said he was chubby and looked as if he got all the sex he wanted and more. He told her she didn't think highly of herself (something I can identify with in myself) and that she carried guilt feelings from the past, which in trying to overcome, she was punishing herself. He asked her if she went out with fellows much. She said no. He asked her if she had any sex life. Maybe, Rose added, once in a while. He told her she needed it and told her to go out to a dance and find a guy or join a young people's group in church. Beth told me she didn't wholly agree with him 'cause if a girl goes out looking for sex and gets it, it might satisfy her to some small physical degree, but it also hurts her sense of dignity, pride and well-being, which not only doesn't help her, but harms her condition. Beth was supposed to go back and see this psychologist again. Instead, she phoned his supervisor and asked if she could have someone else. The supervisor told her they were stretched beyond their ability to handle all who came to them and suggested Beth write out what she felt she wanted to tell. She said she started to do this. Sometimes when Beth looks at me with her big soft brown eyes, I think of a fawn. She has a kind of gentleness that goes with it when she's quiet.

January 3, 1994   Diary to Lauren Morgan

Thoughts of Lauren lurk in the back of my mind as my shadow around me—always there from almost unnoticeable to very obvious. Have idea for TV commercial about Queen Cola (a soft drink):

Scene: King seated on throne, three steps above the court. He is wearing crown, regal robe and has the royal scepter in his right hand. In his left hand, which is extended he holds a can or bottle of Queen Cola. A court jester, wearing the usual clown or jester garb, with silly bobble cap stands below and to his right, with left foot on lower step, right foot on second step, facing the King with his right hand leaning on right thigh. King speaks in deep majestic tones—slow and lordly.

King: Ho! Thou jester! Many praises to thee for recommending this noble drink, Queen Cola—exquisitely pleasurable to the palate, delightfully zesty, Queen Cola is aptly named. Pre-eminent in quality, the Queen of Colas.

Jester: I don't disagree, your majesty; and it is not because I dare not.

King: Other soft drinks may be adequate for some people, but with that uniquely great taste, only Queen Cola is fit for a King.

Jester: Alas, your majesty, it is also fit for the likes of me.

Announcer: Queen Cola—Taste fit for a King, but priced for the crowd.

Will send this off to Queen Cola's Advertising Department.

January 4, 1994   Diary to Lauren Morgan

Had coffee with Beth at table in her room by the open door—a terrific person to drink coffee with. Her married sister, who lives in New Jersey, hasn't been well. She revealed to Beth that she told her husband if anything happens to her, he is to let Beth take care of him. Beth added this was done without her being consulted first.

Showed Beth my TV commercial idea about Queen Cola. She liked it. Told her I didn't think I'd make it as a great writer. She said you never know what hidden power in you might be unleashed for you to go beyond yourself under the right circumstances. People tend to think of you what you think of yourself. She's a good cheer-leader. She knows about life. Wants me to eat more to offset mental energy to be burned up by me. Says she know how it is to feel unnecessary. She, too, feels disturbed because of a sense of being a failure. Likes to reminisce of her younger days in Scotland. Seems like a far-away dream sometimes. She was commenting on when she worked in the hospital there. She thought she was very important then. A funny thing, she said, that when patients she took care of got better, she didn't feel interested in them anymore, only while they needed her. She's a giver.

January 5, 1994   Diary to Lauren Morgan

Lauren contacted me. Said she wants to talk at the Blarney Stone after work. At the Blarney Stone, she said she didn't want me up in the apartment any more. At least, she waited until after Christmas to tell me. The thought of never being alone with her in the apartment again except to hurriedly pick up the rest of my belongings, sickens me. While I had something to eat, she had one beer and left. I got depressed again. Went to my room and in bed got to going over good times with her that might have continued—this and the reality of me in my small crowded room asking myself if it's worth it, all the effort it takes to go on living.

Chapter Sixty

January 6, 1994   Diary to Lauren Morgan

Progress I might have been making in myself in the company of Beth was setback yesterday in the company of Lauren. I don't know if it's two steps forward and one step back, or one step forward and two steps back. Had a dream last night about a man, a symbol of myself, I guess, who apparently from mental wounds, began to protect himself. Against fear he began to put up a defense—a block—to shield him. Later, another block next to it against suspicion, and another against embarrassment, until he was encircled with protective blocks. They were ankle high at first and then he began to pile blocks on top of this foundation against slights, aggression, insults, scorn etc. until they rose above his waist.

While he could still see above these blocks, he discovered love—and with it, some allied feelings, hope, kindness, tenderness, patience, understanding. Changed, he was able to climb over the encircling and restricting blocks towards freedom. The combination of his new feelings and presence of mind, dominating the older protective emotions, created an aura of ecstasy—a sublime euphoria. It was like living on a cloud, knowing only spring, roses and sunshine with possible light rain.

Then somebody happened to change him again. His trust was misplaced, he thought; his love taken too lightly or rejected, he thought. He did not realize couples grow and change and lose their unifying force toward each other. He felt if he did not climb back over the blocks and into his protective shell, he would be more vulnerable. So he found himself back in his fortress.

Now he was bitter, resentful, untrusting, hateful—and hating himself, his weakness most of all. But at least he was protected. And when he regained his composure, he completed the shell, piling up blocks higher and higher and finally, fashioning a curved roof over his head. Now he was safe—he could not be attacked. The only problem was, he couldn't see what was going on outside except through small openings between blocks that gave him only limited vision and no peripheral view. He thought, "Am I living? Would I not be better off dead—gone—nothing?"

He longed for freedom again, for a powerful love that had once given him his release and ecstatic joy for life. Could he risk the hurt again? Maybe next time it would kill him. No. Too risky—can't play with the unknown—too powerful, too uncertain—could be violent annihilation of soul and ego, if not body. He lived like this for a time, with a dichotomy of mind and will. The mind cautioning stay—the will urging to try again in the jungle out there.

This inner battle was tearing him in two—he was miserable. Then, he began to hear a voice, softly at first but powerful, confident and loving. He could not tell if it came from outside the shell, or within it or even if it were not within his own mind. But this voice did not threaten, it did not scold and did not even try to persuade or cajole. It effused a strange, almost supernatural feeling of contentment without knowledge, harmonious joy, and an intuitive certain conviction of truth, unity and goodness. What was this feeling? Whose voice did he hear? Sometimes, he was not even sure it was a voice. It sounded more like the current of a deep river; other times like the mystical harmony of the universe, yet somehow blending into one all-powerful true tonic sound of bliss. His feelings were unable to convey his experience. They could signal vague hints and impressions, but it was like trying to define spirit. His mind was powerless against some unexplained omnipotent, omniscient mystic force that was irresistible and magnetic.

The man was given a new feeling of courage and an insatiable curiosity to discover what he was experiencing. If he was losing his mind, he wanted to know and to know why. The quiet but strong voice he experienced, calmed his fears and gave him confidence such as he had never before known. It could make him feel power and ecstasy and peace, even if he didn't know why. Along with this new powerful force he discovered allied words that in his life had long since fallen into disuse. This feeling cast its rays from without and from inside his soul outward, and lit up paths in all directions and heights and depths. It reached into the deepest and darkest abyss and into reflecting mirrors and prisms of incandescence.

This strange, supernatural metamorphosis of soul, truly a treasure was new to him because it did not seem to benefit him directly. It was not like his old emotion of love for someone else which was expected to be reciprocated. It had nothing of the possessive character of the old passion which sometimes seemed to border on domination and ownership. This new kind of feeling was completely self-abnegating—love of someone or everyone because of superabundance, an overflowing in his own soul—like a river overflowing its banks and irrigating the parched fields adjacent crying out for sustenance.

Perhaps, these descriptions fail to convey his true feelings—probably so. Really, he did not understand these emotions himself and was unable to use words to express the power and sublime joy, the spiritual desire, the courage that his soul, his entire being now encompassed.

This newness he had gained enabled him to push aside his protective fortress and he was free to walk in the world again. He read further, studied, asked, learned, disputed, listened, refuted, argued and grew in knowledge. He studied philosophy, history, philology, science etc., and finally, came to religion. If philosophy confused him with its myriad and contradictory opinions concerning every facet of being, theology seemed to fill him with dismay, consternation and even irritation. The whole world, it seemed to him, was divided into scores of different beliefs and even within the major religious denominations, there were infinite numbers of differences on major and minor points. He was confronted with belief and apparently, strong belief, but belief in what? Religion seemed to be a quagmire, a swamp with inestimable varieties of life, good and wicked, beautiful and ugly, sublime and sordid, all different yet all coexisting, even thriving together. He was confronted, it appeared, with fragmented chaos.

He experienced doubt and something of disillusionment. He was perplexed and wanted someone to tell him which doctrine was correct—which was the right direction. But everyone he asked pointed in different directions. This confusion was undermining his strength and power, weakening his hope, diminishing his joy. He needed truth— the one and only sure truth—but how to find it?

He began to ruminate over the personal philosophies and theories of those men who, in his extensive reading, had most impressed him. He recalled with great delectation the sublime Plato and his Doctrine of Ideas, wherein all worldly objects are merely inept and pitifully inadequate copies. To Plato, the idea of God was that of the perfect planner, the abstract idea of good. What then of his successor, the mighty builder of systematic knowledge—Aristotle? Aristotle conceived of God as the prime driving force, the necessary agent, the immutable and perfect activity. To Epicurus, God was impersonal harmony, the face and order of beauty. The Stoics, Zeno, Seneca, Epictetus, Marcus Aurelius etc., thought God represented the anonymous wisdom and pantheist principle which the presence of the earth, seemed to them to presuppose. Our man was now gathering divergent opinions from the best of the pre-Christian and early Christian philosophers and was still in a muddle.

He recalls an old hero, the peaceful and humble giant, Spinoza, whose philosophy of Pantheism once stirred his soul so deeply. To regard nature, geometric forces as the primary substance; not God is all –but all is God. But what then? John Locke said all is matter. Bishop Berkeley said all was mind. Total disorder reigns. Then comes the skeptic David Hume, who said there is no mind, only a set of individual, disorganized ideas of association. To boot, Hume destroys the law of cause and effect. Hume says, "There's a God? Prove it philosophically and scientifically!"

Our liberated man now weeps a flood of tears. "Help," he cries. He hopefully remembers Chinaman of Konigsberg Emanuel Kant, who wrote volumes of obscurity to repulse the wave of secular and atheistic intellectualism, in order to deny the finality of the intellect in the field of transcendental problems. Kant says intuitive faith is the answer.

Now, the fortress man is completely disoriented and chaos gains dominion over his wits. He rests from his contemplative thoughts and looks at the world around him. It is not he thinks very beautiful. Is art the answer? Why not worship beauty, one of Plato's pure forms? But then, he reflected, did not Platonism eventually merge with Christianity? But what, he wonders, in thinking of Jesus Christ, about Buddha, Confucius, Lao Tzu, Mohammed and the millions of people who worship in these religions? What about Judaism? The Jews have had faith longer than any people. What about the primitive, primal people who worship mother earth? Who is correct? What is right? More disturbed becomes our man.

By now, he is a mental and emotional fracture. Besides that, he is taunted and teased by those insensitive brutes who appear to have found their own personal, smug, comfortable solution. Ridiculed, harassed, embarrassed, he turns once again to a woman for solace. Here, he was accepted and welcomed, but alas briefly, only again to be deceived bitterly. He sees himself as just about finished. He is feeling old and little. Where, he asks, is the voice that once spoke so powerfully to his soul? It is now silent.

He is weary, aware of an amazing force overcoming his fear while he rests, aware of his spirit taking over all of him in his journey from this world into the next world.

Chapter Sixty One

January 7, 1994   Diary to Lauren Morgan

Lauren contacted me. Said I could come to the apartment next week to pick up rest of my belongings. After that, I got to thinking of how famous trials, attended by all ranks and classes, rival theaters; how a man or woman in agony draws crowds—human nature stripped and passions revealed in flashes of love, hate, jealousy and revenge, like that simmering in my brain.

Went to AA meeting and after had coffee with Beth at her table by the open door of her room. When I suggested she sit back in her chair and relax, she said, "I'm used to not making myself as comfortable as I should. I'm not kind to myself—a kind of revenge over the guilt of having an illegitimate baby when I was young in Scotland. The thought of having and losing the baby a week later is with me always." She mentioned another boyfriend she had in Scotland after that who was from another city and very kind to her. "He didn't know I had had an illegitimate baby. I felt I wasn't good enough for him and just broke off our friendship and came to America. I don't think he ever knew why and I think it hurt him. Still, I thought it was the right thing. I preferred to have him remember me as he knew me then. I never would have told him in a million years of having an illegitimate baby with another guy."

Beth calms my thoughts. One of the fellows in the building said Beth reminds him of a little girl that got lost. She's someone you can feel genuine fondness for while feeling she has the same kind of genuine feeling for you. She told me, "When I was working in this country for Mrs. Winger as a baby nurse, she said to me, 'I never met anyone with such a feeling for babies.' And I felt so terrible inside. I couldn't tell her why I had that feeling for babies. She couldn't understand why because I wasn't married and I could take care of her baby the way I did and was so close to it. I was making believe it was my own. I used to take the little baby to my own bed. I got an awful shock when the baby I took care of for another lady in this country got into a convulsion and I thought it was dead. It brought the memory, lifelike, of the illegitimate baby I had in Scotland that only lived a week; they took me up stairs, it was lying on a slab and I was screaming and screaming and screaming. And when I went over to the crib and saw the baby I was taking care of in this country with its eyes up in its head, I thought to myself that if anything happened to it, I would go out of my mind. I was about to end my employment there and I wondered why that should happen to me before I left; and here, the mother of that baby was so grateful that it happened before I left.

Isn't that kind of ironic? (As Beth speaks her voice has a soulful tone which I can associate with music.) That was the last time I took care of babies. I felt it was time for me to stop. That frightened me out of taking care of babies. I was afraid a baby might get sick and die and I couldn't stand to see a dead baby. I was haunted for years and years and years before I would go to sleep and I would see that. When I was sick after that, and I was in a convalescent home and went to a sermon, and minister said, 'Suffer little children to come unto me,' that memory came up again and I went to the ladies room and cried. And that was after all those years. That faded away for a while after I came to this building to live. It was not as vivid as it used to be before the change of life. What etches something in a person's mind so it's like a ghost? 'The Lord giveth and the Lord taketh,' my father said. My baby was taken and I lived and wanted to be taken. When my sister, Isabel, died I thought that wasn't fair. I felt I should have been taken instead of her because she had a husband and children to live for and I didn't have anybody." As Beth said that I thought, why shouldn't I be the one in need of a heart transplant instead of my son?

Chapter Sixty Two

On January 8, 1994 LeMay and Lauren took off again for Mexico-Flying to Tijuana, landing at its International Airport on the eastern edge of the city. When they had booked in at the Pueblo Amigo Holiday Inn, they shopped around in this world's most visited city, as its boosters optimistically proclaim, extending for more than a dozen miles along International border, its downtown core less than a mile from the U.S and about six miles inland from the Pacific- crowded, part flashy, part trashy, drawing hordes of weekend tourists, college-age partiers and dedicated shoppers.

LeMay and Lauren walked along the Avenida Revolution, the main street of Tijuana, some eighteen miles south of San Diego and in the north of the Baja California, having been lost to the U.S. in the Mexican American war of 1848: prohibition fueled tremendous growth as well as Tijuana's sinful reputation for drinking, gambling and you-name-it.

As a free port, foreign merchandise is sold at lower prices than in the U.S or mainland Mexico. Because of its, status as a duty free port of entry, Tijuana offered attractive displays of watches, Russian caviar, Italian shoes, French cosmetics, European designer fashions, Scottish cashmere sweaters,

Oriental rugs, fine crystal, gold jewelry and other international goods as well as Mexican crafts.

While tacos, burritos and enchiladas are in abundant supply, dining options in Tijuana are certainly not limited to them, the city offering a variety of international cuisines. While eating lunch at the Pueblo Amigo, LeMay told Lauren he had, for a long time, wanted to make the trip down the Baja California peninsula, a strip of land extending southward and parallel to the northwestern Mexican mainland, some eight hundred miles long varying from some thirty to one hundred and ten miles in width, bordered by the Pacific to the west and the sea of Cortez to the east. Once the province of pirates launching raids on Spanish galleons from the cover of this peninsula's protected caves, it remained a lonely outpost until well into the twentieth century. Except for a handful of towns and resorts that catered to the well-to-do, it was inhabited mainly by Indians and hardy fishermen. Bringing Baja out of the age, it was in the opening of the trans peninsular Mex 1 in 1973 – the highway from Tijuana to Cabo San Lucas at the southern tip. Not perfectly straight, the highway occasionally crosses from one side of the peninsula to the other. The peninsula remains a last frontier in some ways- isolated from the rest of Mexico. Visitors come to frolic on the white sandy beaches, surf the Pacific Breakers, fish and view the stark inspiring scenery that unfolds away from hotel pools and souvenir shops

After dining, LeMay and Lauren took advantage of the night-life revolving around discos, including stops at Baby Rock and Oh! finding the Zona Rio discos discriminating in that those in jeans and T-shirts weren't able to get in

LeMay and Lauren turned in shortly after midnight at the hotel they had booked, and the following morning went by bus to Ensenada, about sixty miles south of Tijuana along the Pacific Coast, blending the characteristics of a border town with a typical Mexican city of the interior. They noticed between Tijuana and Ensenada, along the beautiful coastlines were many trailer parks and mobile home villages. They were told many Americans have homes along the highway and like living at or near the beach. An English language newspaper, The Baja Times, printed in Tijuana, carries news and items of interest on the whole Baja peninsula. It suggested that if in parts, the heat got to be too much, you do as the locals do- rise early in the morning, take a siesta in the heat of the afternoon, and venture out again in the evening after temperature has cooled off. Occasional flash floods, although rare, have been known to take place in August and September.

Lemay and Lauren continued on through Ensenada to San Ignacio, between a third and half way down the Baja Peninsula, a pretty town – small and quiet, with an old San Ignacio Mission and a plaza with enormous stately trees.

Through San Ignacio, they continued to about half way down and on the east coast of the peninsula toward Mulege with luxury hotels and a landing field. About a mile south of the town was the Oasis Rio Baja trailer park.

Through San Ignacio they continued to about two thirds of the way down the peninsula to Loreto near the east coast, noticing four luxury hotels- one being called the Oasis Hotel. Further on, to about four fifths of the way down the peninsula, they came to LaPaz on the east coast. They could have flown there from Tijuana in an hour and forty minutes, but LeMay wanted to see the sights on the ground. They could have taken a ferry from LaPaz, across the Sea of Cortez, to Mazatlan on the Mexican mainland but LeMay wanted to continue their trip on the ground to the tip of the peninsula.

From the LaPaz area, where there were several trailer parks and tourists could find much of what they wanted, they continued on another one hundred and forty miles south toward Cabo San Lucas at the tip of the peninsula. Ten miles before reaching the cape, they took in the Hotel Cabo San Lucas, its terraced dining rooms overlooking the Sea of Cortez from a rocky promontory, the waves dashing on the rocks fifty feet below. At last, at Cabo San Lucas, they saw the tip of the peninsula where the Pacific Ocean joins the sea of Cortez. Taking a small boating ride out is the crashing of innumerable gulf and ocean waves sculpturing striking rock formations.

Up until a few years ago, Cabo San Lucas was primarily a destination for moneyed sportsmen and those escaping the crowds at Mexico's more established seaside getaways.

Recently, Baja's southern tip had become a destination of choice for the fashionably unshaven who, unlike '80s yuppies and their satanized Club Med tastes, relish southern Baja's non-touristy atmosphere, nearly deserted beaches and prime surfing spots.

At the Hotel Finisterra where LeMay and Lauren were staying, they took advantage of the Whale Watcher's Bar to sip margaritas while watching the sun slowly drop into the Pacific with mariachis playing in the background, followed by meals of fresh sea food.

LeMay and Lauren found Cabo San Lucas had a fairly active night life due to the preponderance of surfer types and other youthful revelers. Rather than the flashy discos common in other Mexican resorts, casual buyers and rock n' rollers were more common elements of life on the town. The Cabo Wabo Cantina with a phallic symbol, capping this watering hole was open until the wee hours. They also went to the Giggling Marlin which had frequent live music, and an attraction there being a pulley device that dangled patrons upside down—rather, like a captured fish—to the amusement of the others.

Returning to the Finisterra Hotel to spend the night, Lauren found some of LeMay's charm turned off. He became sullenly silent while taking from a pocket of his suit-coat a package of opium and giving himself 35 grains, which he said was to sooth his stomach. He offered Lauren some, which she refused. He rested, still and silent while she took a shower and put on clean silk panties. Lauren's manner and form, being a little on the plump side the way he liked women, her black hair, spotless white soft skin, full nicely formed breasts, shapely legs and the way he found himself fully aroused and relieved with her, left an indelible imprint. He became irked when it seemed she talked too much about him when she drank more than was good for her, but it had not stopped his strong want for her. Yet, it bothered him she made remarks of him representing rappers who were connected with drugs and the Mafia. He mentioned it to her there. She said she was sorry while thinking of him as a type of man who only wanted a woman, when he wanted her, and when he wanted her, it was with a fierce want, as though making up for not always having her. He was not a lover flitting from flower to flower. He was hooked on Lauren and seemed content to give things a chance to shape themselves.

Chapter Sixty Three

After catching some sleep at the Finisterra Hotel, LeMay and Lauren took the ferry from Cabo San Lucas across the sea of Cortez to Puerto Vallarta, about mid-way down the west coast of the Mexican mainland—a village with crowded, not too wide streets, and hotels in abundance, in an area of alluring beauty with its coastline of broad, sandy beaches and off-shore islands, combining a leisurely, slow-paced ambience with fun, dining and flashy nigh life.

After getting off the ferry at Puerto Vallarta, LeMay and Lauren looked around the city and took a plane to Guadalajara, the nation's second largest city. They checked in at the Presidente Inter-Continental Guadalajara Hotel and went for some Mexican food at a nearby restaurant, where they met an American couple, Ed and Helen Swenson, seeming to be in their late sixties and in good health.

"We're just a couple of Americanos that came down here to retire," Ed said.

"Thirteen years ago," Helen added.

"The big attraction?" Ed asked and answered. "High on the list is the climate. It's claimed more Americans live in Guadalajara than in any other foreign city in the world."

"What do you recommend we see?" LeMay asked.

"Take a stroll through the Plaza de la Liberacion between the Cathedral and the Degollado Theatre, or the Plaza de las Armas in front of the National Palace," Ed answered. "Attractions such as the tree-lined streets in the Chapalita or Country Club sections or the fountains along Chapultepec make Guadalajara one of the most beautiful cities in country."

"The suburbs of the Tlaquepaque and Tonala and the villages along nearby Lake Chapala, the largest inland lake in Mexico, enhance the area," Helen added.

"Many beautiful real estate developments are in progress near Chapala."

We have driven out to the United States several times and not been attacked or threatened," Helen continued after her husband.

"One time when we were driving in the country at night, a herd of cattle crossed the highway in front of us. Luckily, Helen was going less than 25 miles an hour."

"We have lived on the same block," Helen continued, "with the same friendly Mexican neighbors many years and feel safe walking alone at night. Although I did have my billfold stolen on a sightseeing tour somewhere else in the country. I could never figure out how anyone got it out of my bag because I always had a hard time finding it myself."

"We do have pickpockets and some burglars," Ed added, "but they don't carry guns, which are harder to get here than in the U.S. Mexico has no National Rifle Association. As long as you aren't into drugs, you're safe here."

"We are not into drugs," LeMay said.

"At least I'm not," Lauren added.

"With almost perfect climate the year around and low cost living, on American dollar income, this is the answer for us retirees—closer to paradise than any other place or situation we know of."

"A lot of English is spoken here and it's not hard to pick up the Spanish spoken here," Helen added.

"Over eighty organizations in our area are in English, including eight churches, American legion, American Society, Memorial Society, book club, bridge club, dinner club, singles club…"

"Some of us are busier than before we retired," Helen said.

"We have seen most of Mexico—a land of contrasts, from snow-covered mountain tops to canyons, plains, deserts and all the water you could ask for."

"Been down the Baja Peninsula?" LeMay asked.

"We'll consider that for our next jaunt," Ed answered.

LeMay and Lauren went on to mention something of what they had experienced going down the Baja Peninsula.

Helen went to say, "We have exchanged homes and hospitality around the world two dozen times and visited over thirty countries. After seeing the Great Pyramid show at Cairo, Egypt, we both say it's not as good as the show at Uxmal. The pyramids of Egypt are not nearly as picturesque as those of Uxmal, Chichen, Itza, Palenque and Teotihuacan."

"I have a brother, a bachelor," Ed said, "who seems as at odds with himself in retirement as he was before retiring. I told him to come down here where I can eat out at least twice a week in gourmet restaurants and not be shocked at the cost. For our home and my wife, a maid would be nice…"

"If a maid were hired, it would not be for me. I've made it clear to him we do not need a maid."

"Anyway, our home has a patio with flowers and a small pool, a fountain and goldfish and a satellite antenna to get my TV in English."

Lauren asked LeMay, "Had you thought of getting a place down here?"

"There's something to be said for it," LeMay answered.

"He," Helen said while indicating her husband," never wears a tie and suit coat now, except to a wedding or funeral."

"If you want radio news in English, bring a good shortwave radio. Cords with grounded three-prong plugs won't plug into outlets here without an adapter. Plug-in electric clocks do not keep perfect time here."

"You're smart to come down here for a vacation first before moving down. You could visit the American Society," Helen suggested. "I have been impressed by the giant strides the American Society of Jalisco has made in providing cultural activities for its members. It also sponsors worthwhile charitable programs for those who wish to participate in constructive work for Mexican children and their families. We had volunteered to cover the cost of quinceanera of a young Mexican girl—an event celebrated on the fifteenth birthday of a young Latin American girl, announcing to the world that she would now be of age to participate in social events enjoyed by her elders. The event was held at the girl's home from which, one hundred people were invited. A record player or orchestra was to provide the music. The former was used since it could be used for entertainment after the fiesta was over."

"Also needed was a camera to take pictures of the event," Ed added.

"Next was the girl's dress. She had been through her first Communion at age eight, when she was dressed like a bride with a white gown, gloves, shoes, tiara and corsage. Now was a repetition, only on a grander scale. I shopped throughout the city and found an economical store selling wedding dresses, like those worn at quinceaneras."

"Some families got through this by taking out a mortgage on their homes," Ed added. "Into the pictures comes the church with a High Mass specially given for the girl, calling for flowers in abundance. Debatable is, if the ritual of quinceaneras was started as a source of income for the church and florists. Also in the ceremony was a red runner up the aisle, a full-blown chorus, pads on which the girl, her parents and escort knelt during the one hour service and a fee for the priest performing the Mass and another fee for the Mass itself."

"At that point, I was asking for a glass of water and a bottle of aspirin," Helen added.

"Our horoscope must have been favorable for that day because we learned some of the expense we were expected to take care of would be taken over by a relative of the girl for the many other requirements," Helen again added, "with the young girl finally going to bed around 6 a.m.

Ed added, "I guess what we learned from this was, we could still party all night."

"Run into much rapping down here" LeMay asked.

"I hear more of that over the radio from American stations than down here," Ed answered.

"With a publicity blitz, they could come to appreciate rapping down here the way we do in New York," said LeMay.

"Hopefully without gangsta identification," Lauren added.

"It's always there, waiting to be expressed—where you came from, what you've experienced,"LeMay added.

"You into rap?" Ed asked.

"I tried being a rapper, but wasn't top notch at it. I discovered those who were, and got to managing some of them."

"He's into it about as much as you can be in it," Lauren said.

"What she means is, as well as handling rappers, I own a record company, TV station, movie studio and other publicity devices to help my rappers on their way," LeMay added.

"What do you expect the new rappers will come out with?" Ed asked.

"I visualize a kind of surrealistic painting with words. Art imitating life as the artist sees it. Still, rap rivalry is competitive –some healthy, some not. A whole industry is turned into hustle to get the hottest piece, artist and act and turn it into a lot of money."

"He listens for the next big beat and the words to go with it," Lauren added.

"Rap could do with a little sexy humor. I received something recently which I'm thinking of having recorded. It's called "My Whim." LeMay took a folded sheet of paper out of his pocket and passed it to the others.

MY WHIM

I am a girl with many a fault,
In many ways not worth my salt.
I can neither cook nor sew,
I'd never make a household go.
But in one thing I do excel,
As many a man can truly tell.
I was young when I began,
Taught by a most attractive man.
Young and strong and full of vim,
I surely learned a lot from him.
At first I was so very shy
It seemed a dangerous thing to try.
Practice soon perfected my art,
Now I'm paid to do my part.
And now in open competition,
I feel I have no opposition.
No matter if it's rain or shine,
It's still a favorite sport of mine.
Why should I not indulge my whim—
Which after all is just to swim?

"It has been suggested, the rapping could be done by someone like a talented centerfold playgirl," LeMay added.

"She wouldn't necessarily have to be all naked. She could have her shoes on," Ed also added.

The two couples exchanged addresses before parting.

LeMay and Lauren visited some of the places Ed and Helen had suggested and in the evening stopped off at the lobby bar of the American Hotel with its classy club/lounge with live music, LaDiligencia in the Camino Real Hotel with its romantic atmosphere for music and dancing and Maxim's Disco in the Hotel Frances.

Shortly after midnight, they returned to the Presidente Inter-Continental Guadalajara Hotel, where after undressing, she took a shower, while he gave himself 35 grains of opium.

When Lauren had finished her shower and put on clean silk panties, he said, "I didn't like it when after I told the Swensons a publicity blitz down here could bring the area to appreciate rapping the way they do in New York, you said, "Hopefully without gangster identification.' It inferred I might be connected with gangsters. And to make it worse you also said, after I mentioned I got to managing rappers, that I was into it as much as anybody can be into it,' which inferred the same thing again."

"You aren't reading things into what I said?"

"I'm reading what others can read in between the lines. I'm not going to keep warning you."

"All right, all right."

The nigh was finished off with him hugging her with tears in her eyes, after which he rolled over and dozed off to sleep.

The following day, they flew back to New York City.

Chapter Sixty Four

January 8, 1994   Diary to Lauren Morgan

While having coffee with Beth at the table in her room by the open door, she said Lauren told her LeMay takes opium. He had told Lauren stomach pains had driven him to take opium for relief. The result had seemed phenomenal to him and his pain ceased and he knew boundless pleasure. I feel sorry for Lauren—she who has told me she feels sorry for me! I go to sleep with her image, wake up in the night with it, start the day with it, take it to work with me, bring it home with me…I blame myself, losing my job from too much drinking, getting to be unemployed nuisance around the apartment, which Lauren tolerated 'til revenge aggravation set in and she picked an argument with me that got out of hand, so she and her front teeth parted company… Don't know what I'd do without Beth—I feel blessed having her next door as I exist among the ruins of my life—bewildered, dazed, crushed. I told Beth, that in a world where one can hunger for friendship, I feel fortunate to have her, who understands the conflict between aspirations and actuality and the way things happen that disappoint, injure and destroy. When we have coffee together, she's not with me as a spectator of my misfortune, but as someone truly caring and helpful.

Chapter Sixty Five

Mark's wife, Sandra, and Rina, after jogging together, approached Sheldon's gym, as Sam asked, "How far did you run today?"

"Two miles," Rina answered.

"Same here," Sandra added."

Not forgetting to throw punches to the wind along the way and bobbing, ducking and weaving?" Sam asked.

"Not forgetting," Rina said.

Two other girls with head protector, chest protector and boxing gloves on, approached Sam, who said, "Melinda and Kim, meet Sandra."

After acknowledgements Melinda, tall and thin, and Kim, shorter and stout, got in the ring. "Two 2 minute rounds," Sam said, "OK start." While watching with Sandra and Rina, Sam said, "Those two aren't as experienced as Rina. Each of them is showing so much respect for the other, the action is almost defensive on the part of each."

At the end of first round, Sam called Melinda and Kim to him at the side of the ring and said, "Your action reminds me of two male world class fighters—facing each other with so much respect for each other, there's not much of a fight. OK, try again." Melinda and Kim then went at each other in an almost no-holds-barred manner. After watching them, Sam said, "OK, that's enough. If you two fight like that in a scheduled outside competition, you could be disqualified. There's such a thing as rules. You don't hit an opponent on the back or the back of the neck. No butting or elbow blows. No hitting with the open glove. No holding and hitting. No hanging on to an opponent. No wrestling. OK, give your head and chest gear and gloves to Rina and Sandra."

While Melinda and Kim handed over their boxing gear to Rina and Sandra, Rina said, "Lay people don't understand much of women in boxing."

"In their minds," Kim added, "boxing's brutal and violent and only killers do it."

"They don't understand," Rina continued, "the science and fun of the sport and the good it does for young kids coming off the street and gaining discipline."

"When you're in the ring, it's you on your own," Kim said.

"You make decisions and react in split seconds, "Rina added. "Often, a lot of it is subconscious and the work you do on the heavy bag and running for stamina is homework."

Sandra said she liked the environment there—a woman in a man's world.

"You can get addicted to this," Rina added.

"OK," said Sam, "Rina will be doing a little more than just protecting herself, Sandra. She'll be hardly more than tapping you. Understood?"

"Understood," said Rina as she and Sandra got into the ring.

"Two 2-minute rounds. Go."

Rina went at Sandra, bobbing and weaving, tapping a few times, backing off and going forward, bobbing and weaving and dancing from side to side. "Take it easy, Rina," Sam cautioned.

Sandra went at Rina, getting in punches of her own. "Ok, rest." Sam walked to Sandra's corner. "You're letting yourself be a standing target while she bobs and weaves in and out and around you, try bobbing and weaving around her, in and out, from side to side."

Sandra and Rina went through a second 2-minute round, with Sandra showing some, if slight, progress. "Ok that's it. Take a shower," Sam said.

The four women went into a dressing room where, while proceeding to undress to take a shower, Melinda said, "The world outside is more skeptical than the people in the gym here."

"Boxing's not like in the old days," voiced Rina. "Then, there was one champ in each of eight weight divisions, from bantamweight to heavyweight. Today, you have champ titles everywhere you look. And at weigh-ins today, twenty-four hours before a fight, you can come up ten to twenty pounds heavier between then and the time of the fight. Because of this, we have lightweights looking like middleweights."

"If women can box, they should have a say in how boxing should be run," Sandra added.

Chapter Sixty Six

January 13, 1994   Diary to Lauren Morgan

Lauren contacted me in the middle of morning and said I could come up to apartment on Saturday for a couple of hours and tonight would meet me at Blarney Stone with mail for me that had come to the apartment. When I met her after work, at Blarney Stone she was very nice. Told her of things I'm taking from the apartment. She offered to help me. After she left, I felt very relieved that I didn't get angry and upset as I had expected. I still care for her. Thinking of writing a letter of my feelings for her. Feel a wonderful relief of depression because she was kind and said if I wasn't so bad we would have been together forever.

January 14, 1994   Diary to Lauren Morgan

Went to hospital to see about money I owe them. Was told the $2,300 bill could be reduced to $1,600—a complete fouled-up mess. Bad feelings against Lauren returned after I got to thinking of her in the apartment, that she lets LeMay come to in comfort and be able to drink and watch cable TV, while eating a good cooked dinner by Lauren, while I'm confined to my small room with not enough space to hold all my belongings. Went to Al Anon meeting, where I hear usual tales of unmanageable lives. One girl, Sue, said she had been dry for two months and without a job for a month. Said she was a cashier in a large restaurant and could see no reason why the boss fired her, adding, "I'm human being, but you would never know it from the way this boss treated me, using obscenities and threats, the likes of which I haven't experienced before. I got angry. That slime bag boss had no right to treat me like that. I called his home one night after and asked if Gus, that was his name, was in. The woman who answered the phone said he was not in but that she was his wife and would take a message. Then I made believe I was gasping and sounding horrified saying, 'No, no, he never told me he was married! I swear it! Oh God! I wouldn't have done it with him if I had known he was married. And now I'm pregnant. I'm going to have his baby—oh, what am I going to do?' Then I hung up."

"Were you pregnant from him?"

"Certainly not. After that, I called back several times and hung up when the wife answered. About two weeks later, I heard through the grapevine that this former boss's wife had left him and was filing for divorce 'cause he had gotten one of his girlfriend's pregnant."

January 15, 1994   Diary to Lauren Morgan

Went to see Lauren at apartment this Saturday morning. Cleared out a bureau, put more clothes in suitcase. Got stereo record player, books, and shoes. While clearing out things, I got depressed, especially holding the cats. Having coffee before leaving, I told Lauren I still love her. She doesn't love this new guy she's with. Took taxi with more of my belongings to my small room. Whole past with Lauren, eating at me. As

I can't stand being confined with depression, went to Blarney Stone. When I got back to room, became extremely depressed again. Not enough room for all my belongings. Went through poetry I had written to women I had known exclusive of my wife and Lauren, what a waste.

January 21, 1994   Diary to Lauren Morgan

A disturbing week. Had a dream about a sex club for singles in a big house where I'm watching through window. Don't get meaning unless, I prefer to watch now than participate. Found depression gets worse when sun goes down. Many thoughts of Lauren, apartment, and cats. Bad for health. Thoughts of moving out last pieces of my stuff from the apartment almost destroy me because that could be the end of my going there. In middle of the week, Wednesday, contacted Lauren. She said I could come to the apartment Saturday morning to pick up rest of my belongings. Went to chest clinic. Saw new doctor (middle age, seems competent, had black hair but gray beard, which makes him look much older). After that, sought out Welfare information. After long wait, saw man—not bad, quick and efficient. Gave me pile of papers to read. Would have to go to job placement. Would have to go to work-training or something else taking up time. Need letter from last place of work. My first judgment is Welfare isn't worth all the time and trouble. Had bad dream in which everything was fatal frustration and tension for me.

January 22, 1994   Diary to Lauren Morgan

Apprehension going to apartment today—loneliness in sorting and moving out rest of things. Got to apartment around 11 am. Greeted cats. After a while, I gave Lauren a hateful stare loaded with venom. Threatened her with, "You're going to the hospital." Later on I said to her, "I despise you with every fiber of my being." Fondled cats, packed records, two speakers, bathroom cabinet, slide projection machine. I threw out some old suits which are too big and need too much tailoring and out of style; also sweaters and old show records. Lauren helped me with packing, for which I didn't know whether to thank, or condemn her. In the middle of the afternoon, I told her I'd take as much as I could back to my room but would have to come back one more time for a final removal of belongings. She asked how many final removals I had in mind. "One," I said and left with a load of my stuff. Took taxi to my room. Feel big urge to drink.

Chapter Sixty Seven

On a hospital visit to his son, who had been transferred to Columbia-Presbyterian hospital, Mark bumped into his wife, Sandra, who was also visiting the boy. Mark, noticing her face was swollen, asked, "What happened to your face?"

"Why?"

"It looks swollen."

"From boxing," Sandra answered.

"Boxing?"

"From meeting Rina while jogging, and her showing me to the gym where she trains. I got to doing exercises they do, including shadow boxing, and then boxing."

"I hope your brains are not, like your face, swollen," Mark said. "Why do you box?"

"Helps me release feelings of frustration. Hitting the heavy bag is good for getting rid of some stress."

"You like that?"

"I liked the atmosphere of stuffed leather, punching bags, quick shuffling feet, dancing around, bobbing, ducking and weaving, perspiring with focused concentration, blocking shots."

"And taking them… If I did to you what your opponents do you'd have me arrested."

"Boxing gives women the opportunity to express their fighting spirit," Sandra told him.

Chapter Sixty Eight

January 12, 1994   Diary to Lauren Morgan

Unsettled feeling. Went to AA meeting at noon, reminded of Allan Churchill's comment that even though he was dry for two years, he made himself go to Al Anon for his mood and bad frame of mind. After work went over to Billy's Budd's and looked in the window. From there, went to Blarney Stone where an attorney asked me how I'm doing with Lauren. I told him I didn't seem to be able to do anything about my depression over her. He said he had a case where he's trying to defend a guy whose wife shot him because she found out he had been secretly mixing birth control pills with her vitamin pills for twenty years. He didn't want to have kids. She did, very much so; say it was her whole reason for living. After having gotten to be forty-five, when it was too late for her to have kids, and finding out what he had been doing, she shot him. She's being charged with manslaughter, while at the same time she's filing for divorce from him. He made it clear to her that he didn't want kids when they married. She thought she could get around that by punching pinholes in his condoms.

Each was out to outsmart the other. Feeling he had outsmarted her, she shot him. Thought of this, as what can happen when emotions get to an explosion point as I walked to across the street from Billy's Bud's. Bar seemed full. Went to my room.

Chapter Sixty Nine

January 25, 1994   Diary to Lauren Morgan

Unable to make mind transfer contact to Lauren in the afternoon. Phoned her office and was told she had not come in today. I phoned her apartment. There was no answer. She was on my mind the rest of the day.

January 26, 1994   Diary to Lauren Morgan

Still unable to make mind transfer contact to Lauren. Phoned her office in the middle of the morning. Was told she had not come in. I phoned her apartment. No answer. I called her office again an asked if she had taken a few days off. Word from her office was that she had not informed them she would be taking time off yesterday and today. After work, I talked it over with Beth. I wondered if Lauren had gone on a trip with LeMay; but she had always done that on a week-end. If she had gone on a trip on working week-days, she would have let her office know she wasn't coming in.

"I hope she's all right," Beth said. "It's good to be concerned. You can never tell. One of the ladies I worked for, committed suicide and took her two children with her—Winnifred Rockefeller."

"You worked for a Rockefeller?" I asked.

"I looked after her first baby girl, the only child she had at that time. The baby's birthday was the same time as mine. We celebrated together. Then, another baby came along that was sick—kidney trouble. When the second baby came along and I would pick it up, the first baby used to scream and cry. The first baby thought I belonged to her only."

"Who was Winnifred Rockefeller married to?"

"The last name of Winnifred Rockefeller's husband was Emeny. He was a professor of international relations and taught at Yale. She used to read to him. He was sort of stuck-up, stiff-shirted, very polite—seemed more English than American. He used to drive me to the train, put the luggage on the rack and see the window was right. He always treated me like a lady. He was quite impressed with the Rockefeller name. He was quite handsome. She was sensitive and proud, not stuck up. She could be a little distant but she wasn't stuck up. On the maid's night out, she would do the dishes herself. I think he went with other women. He lectured around a lot. It was about twenty five years after then that I read that Winnifred Rockefeller killed herself and two of the children."

"How?"

"By letting the car ran in the closed garage while they were in it. God, she was the last person in the world I thought would do that. I remember when the second baby came along and it was a girl, her husband didn't seem to like it. He wanted a boy and she had two more girls. Maybe she took the two girls with her because she didn't think he wanted them. She used to keep a budget and keep track of the money. She tried to be a housewife, as if she were playing house. She had one maid and me. She took care of her first baby herself for a while but all of her friends started to talk about it. He and she had seemed to be crazy about each other. She was interested in his career; very studious as he was. It was the biggest shock I ever got in my life when I read she killed herself and kids. For about a whole week, I couldn't get over it. I couldn't get it out of my head. She seemed so sensible. If it had been her sister I could have understood; she was sick and a little scatterbrained. Winnifred Rockefeller had written me the most beautiful letter when her first daughter, Betty died. You would have thought Betty was mine. I remember I got Betty a little raincoat with a hood from Scotland and she was so thrilled with it and had her picture taken in it. Winnifred Rockefeller knew the music I liked and used to play it for me on the player piano. And when my sister came to see me, she made us tea without calling the maid—she did it all herself. And when we all went to Ohio, she took Betty in with her so I could get some sleep."

"What did Betty die of?"

"Kidney trouble. She was a doll; and clever. Before she was two years old, she went to nursery school; and she would hang up her coat and hat and put them on the locker by herself. She was such a good little thing. I just adored her; very possessive. She just thought I belonged to her. And when the second baby came along and I picked it up, it broke Betty's heart. Betty had a little thing to teach her to walk and I steadied her to walk without it and she took five steps toward her mother, Winnifred, who almost died of excitement, saying, 'Good girl, good girl,' and picked her up and hugged her. I was with that family for about two years and when I went to work for another family, Winnifred Rockefeller came to see me and the other family was so impressed. I'll remember Winnifred Rockefeller forever."

After talking to Beth, I listened to classical music and well into the evening, went up to Lauren's apartment and rang the bell. No answer. The apartment was dark. I looked in the bar across the street to see if Lauren or LeMay were there. Neither was. I decided to contact the police.

Got in touch with the 19th Precinct Station, telling of my unsuccessful efforts to get in touch with Lauren Morgan at her apartment and at her place of work. I was asked what my relationship to Lauren was. I said I had lived with her for a year and that for almost half a year we had not been living together, although we had kept in touch. He asked me if Lauren Morgan had been living with anyone else since living with me. I said Sellner LeMay had been living with her on and off for the past few months. I was asked to describe LeMay, which I did from what I had seen of him.

"What was his occupation?" I was asked by the detective.

"I don't know."

"What other address does LeMay have?"

"I don't know."

"Do you know if he's married?"

"No."

"Did he have a key to Ms. Morgan's apartment?"

"I assume he did."

"Do you have a key to her apartment?"

"Not since we ceased living together, the locks being changed at that time."

"You don't have a photo of LeMay?"

"No."

"Would any of LeMay's belongings be in Ms. Morgan's apartment?"

"I assume so."

The detective went with me to Lauren's apartment. No one was there. The Superintendent of the building was contacted. He had a key to Lauren's apartment. The door was opened. The two cats in the apartment, which looked as if it needed cleaning, were frightened and hungry. I hugged them and gave them something to eat. I asked the owner if he would look after them until I could. He said he would.

There were items of clothing in the room which LeMay had been occupying. "This is all LeMay's?" the detective asked.

"Some of the belongings in here are mine," I said.

"Yours?"

"Some of my stuff which was still to be removed from the apartment from my breakup with Lauren Morgan."

The detective made some comment about it being strange that belongings of mine and LeMay were in the apartment, from which Lauren Morgan is alleged to be missing. I said I was to have moved the last of my belongings out in a few days. I was asked when was the last time I had been to the apartment before this. I said, "Three days ago, to remove belongings of mine."

Also in the room was a photo of LeMay and Lauren together, which the detective took to make a copy of for an all points bulletin of missing person. The detective looked through drawers to see if any papers or cards could be found. There did not appear to be any of myself or LeMay.

The detective said something to the effect that LeMay could be away with Lauren somewhere. When I mentioned that I had checked with Lauren Morgan's office and they had not received any word from her that she would not be coming in for a few days, the detective said the two of them may possibly have been drinking and on the spur of the moment, decided to take off for somewhere without telling anyone.

Later as the detective and I left the apartment, he said they would see what they could be found out about LeMay and Lauren Morgan through their computer and elsewhere. He also suggested I not leave town.

I didn't like admitting some of the belongings in the apartment were mine. Should I have? The detective could have found out anyway, possibly by seeing not all of the pants, jackets and suits were of the same size—the smaller size of which could fit me, which an alert detective could discover. Why couldn't all of my belongings in that apartment have been removed before this? Taking my time in removing my belongings had been my main excuse for being able to visit Lauren at the apartment and I was trying to string it out as long as possible.

Chapter Seventy

January 29, 1994   Diary to Lauren Morgan

Mood bad. Fear, frustration, anger and annoyance with Lauren missing.

Harder for me to get up yesterday morning. Went to job placement center. Polite, colored lady tried hard to please me. I faked it saying I was waiting to go back to my last job. After work, went to AA meeting. Keep thinking of Lauren missing since Tuesday—four days. And LeMay not located yet.

January 30, 1994   Diary to Lauren Morgan

Little energy. Tried to rearrange my stuff in my small room for more space. Not much to show it. Thinking of Welfare and crime gave rise to idea for a story about crime leading to free education:

Take a man who is ideologically confused, lacking a purpose in life, drifting, but who is intensely curious, yearning to discover some philosophical, ultimate truth—a reason for living, some purposeful direction, a spiritual goal.

He realizes that only through reading the great writers, philosophers, poets and understanding the casual significances in history, culture, politics, ethics, theology, aesthetics can he begin to form his own particular personal ethic by distilling this vast base of knowledge into his own elixir of life, his private plan, method and purpose for being, and through this purpose, this force of direction which impels him to mold his own destiny and pursue it despite all odds and opposition.

Lacking the financial security to quit work and lacking the time, vigor and discipline needed to read, study and reflect while occupied with work, he decided to let the State support his enormous philosophical and cultural undertaking to provide the foundation of knowledge necessary to complete his project.

He therefore, formulates his plan to commit a crime measured to give him a prison term of five years of uninterrupted education, which he feels is sufficient to form the necessary base of knowledge required for his task.

February 4, 1994   Diary to Lauren Morgan

Dragged myself to the office for a few hours on Monday, Tuesday and Wednesday, with Lauren on my mind all the time. Looking at different angles, wonder if possible, LeMay could be with Lauren somewhere alive or killed in a car crash or an air crash. Nothing in the media about a big air crash.

Could it have been in a small plane that went down? Not all small plane or car crashes are splashed around the media.

Worse fear and worry yesterday. Lauren not found. In the afternoon, boss at office asked if I was drinking. I got annoyed and told him if he couldn't tell, then it didn't matter and made no difference. He said he wasn't sure if I was at times, by the way I acted. I wondered if I should tell him about the problems I'm going through because of Lauren. He probably would have said, "Was the pleasure she brought you worth all of what you've gone through?" Decided not to.

Had strange dream before I woke up this morning about being in a boat with another guy and two women who seemed to want money for sex. Dream ended before anything happened. Don't know what it means unless it's that my sexual stamina is not enough to last a dream. After work, went to Al Anon meeting where a girl spoke and said, now that she's getting over her addiction to alcohol, she's going with a man who wants to get married now but there's a problem because "he says when he retires in twelve years he wants to move to Arizona and buy a ranch. But I don't like Arizona. We went there on our last vacation and I didn't like it. I'm a city girl that likes people and noise and the theatre. I don't know how I can marry somebody that wants to end up in a totally different place." Some guy in the audience raised his hand, which she acknowledged. He said to her, "Since the guy that wants to marry you now isn't planning on moving for a dozen years, go for it, because with today's divorce rate, you'll be lucky if your marriage lasts twelve years."

Chapter Seventy One

February 7, 1994   Diary to Lauren Morgan

Stayed in bed much of the weekend, feeling boxed in. Had another strange dream: At some hotel, with bar overlooking the water, talking to a young girl, well-proportioned with a pretty baby face. I told her she looked like a robin or a sparrow. She objected. I said, "You're very young—how old, sixteen?" she said, "I'm a he," and left for guys waiting in a car. Can't figure the meaning unless it's a girl untruthfully saying she's a he to avoid my company.

Today I heard from the detective at the 19th Precinct that LeMay had been contacted.

"Alive?" I asked.

"Yes."

"Where?"

"Mexico City."

"Was Lauren with him?"

"No, she's still missing."

"How long was LeMay in Mexico City?"

"Two weeks?"

"During the time that Lauren has been missing?"

"Yes."

"You have proof?"

"We're checking into that. We'll be in further touch."

February 19, 1996   Diary to Lauren Morgan

Gloomy week in which I toyed with the idea of controlled drinking. Lauren still missing. Detective says a check was made regarding LeMay being in Mexico City. He was there the two weeks he said he was, according to airline ticket check-up. After talking to the detective, I questioned myself about it being a coincidence LeMay was out of the country through the time Lauren has been reported missing. I purposely didn't voice this to the detective. I don't want to give him any hint I might suspect LeMay of anything at present. It could get back to LeMay through the detective mentioning any suspicious comment I might make, giving LeMay a reason to get back at me. I first wanted to see if LeMay would start mentioning suspicious comments against me, which might indicate his possible guilt in the disappearance of Lauren—it being made to look as though I did it. Then again, would it be more effective with the detective if I first make suspicious comments concerning LeMay before he had a chance to make them about me? Maybe LeMay already had and the detective was keeping quiet about it.

February 25, 1996   Diary to Lauren Morgan

A weird week with weird dreams. In one dream was self-levitation—I could move myself, while being horizontal, up to the ceiling. Feel like maybe I'm coming down with something. Possibly some kind of virus. Went to AA meeting where I heard a powerful speaker with his story of helplessness even after he went dry for ninety days, going back on booze and cocaine for six weeks, then to the hospital for a week and back to AA for four months. An edge he has on me is he's only thirty, smart in other ways, good looking and can start over again.

Lauren not found. Detective called me and said LeMay told him Lauren Morgan had said I had a drinking problem.

"I did have. I haven't had a drink for over 100 days," I told him.

He said LeMay had told him Lauren had let him know the reason she broke off with me after living with her for some time was because I knocked her front teeth out.

It being obvious now, LeMay is out to throw suspicion on me, I said, "It's not only told out of context, it's being twisted to give you the impression I'm given to being violent, which I'm not. What happened was Lauren came in drunk one night when we were living together and became aggressive against me with foul language, pointing her finger at me, six inches from my face and pushing me. While holding my hands up to protect my face, she ran into the back of my hand and somehow, two of her upper front teeth were knocked loose." In my wrath of the moment, I thought of saying, how do we know LeMay couldn't have arranged for a hit man to take care of Lauren for him while he was out of the country, but didn't. I said instead, "Did LeMay tell you where he gets his money from?"

"No."

"Lauren had mentioned he was into drugs."

"He took drugs or was involved in the sale?"

"He took opium. I don't know about involvement of him in the sale of drugs."

"Does he have Mafia friends? Mafia enemies?"

"None I can name."

"That's not proof."

Chapter Seventy Two

March 4, 1994   Diary to Lauren Morgan

Unsettled feeling. At office, one of the guys said the boss will put me on regular payroll soon. Went to Al Anon meeting at noon again. Again, reminded of Allan Churchill's comment that even though he was dry for two years, he made himself go for his mood and bad frame of mind.

Was contacted by the detective who said Lauren still missing and that LeMay had told him Lauren Morgan had told him she had had me arrested and had to have a court order drawn up restraining me from living in her apartment and from going near her. I said she had it done as a result of the first big argument we had. The detective asked if Lauren was known to have taken any drugs, which LeMay is alleged to have access to. I said I doubted it because she had mentioned LeMay had asked her if she wanted to try, and she had said she didn't. I added that Lauren did have a drinking problem, which seemed to make more out-going her already out-going nature when in bars drinking, which LeMay had not ceased to notice, and Lauren had mentioned to Beth that LeMay had warned her that if she didn't restrain some of her talk about him, she could be silenced.

"Who is Beth?" the detective asked.

"An elderly lady, living in the next room to where I now live, who had visited with Lauren a number of times."

"I may want to talk to her," the detective said.

March 5, 1994   Diary to Lauren Morgan

Another dream: Living in the country house by a lake, with two cats. I am with woman who had English accent. Then, I'm in a movie house trying to get away from big bearded guy who wants to fight me. When I woke up, tried to figure out what it meant. Two cats could be two cats in Lauren's apartment. The house could be the apartment; the woman I'm with could be Lauren; the big bearded guy could be LeMay. Later, went to an Al Anon meeting where a girl said to me after, "Have you noticed about the quality of service lately? I went into a boutique. I asked the sales girl if she had any more of my size in black. She said, 'I dunno.' When I asked if she could check, she said, 'No.' no explanation, not even a 'Sorry'. We have to accept that service is getting dead in the U.S. these days. If you want real service, you've got to go to Asia."

Chapter Seventy Three

March 11, 1994   Diary to Lauren Morgan

A blue week in which I went to see my son. No heart donor for him has been forthcoming. Asked guy at office about boss's plans for me. Said I might be on payroll after we move. Get annoyed over boss keeping me in suspense.

Detective asked me if I violated court restraining order against me. I said it was only after getting Lauren's permission first. Detective said that was violation. He added, "LeMay says Lauren had told him you had said to her in an argument, 'I will kill you,' which was attested to by arresting officers. In what context or sequence of events was that made?"

I said, "It would have been in a second argument I had with Lauren. We had a big argument a week before that, because festering in her was my having lost my job through drinking and hanging around the apartment, out of which I was arrested then for a day."

"At which time Lauren Morgan had a court order drawn up restraining you from living in her apartment or going near her?"

"Yes. Then, because I had no place to go after being arrested for a day, she allowed me to live with her another week and at the end of that week, we had the second big argument when we said things to each other we should not have."

"With you saying, 'I will kill you?'"

"Yes."

"You were jailed again?"

"Yes."

"Where?"

"Rikers Island."

"For how long?"

"Twenty days."

How much more did Lauren tell LeMay about us that he can tell the detective? Could she have told him about my putting Ajax powder in her plant?"

Chapter Seventy Four

Sandra and Rina, who had been jogging again, made their way into Sheldon's gym. After resting a little, they went through bending, push-ups and other forms of exercising, followed by shadow boxing. Sandra was not boxing with anyone, she was just shadow boxing.

Sam, standing by, noticed Sandra's effort grow almost negligible, followed by Sandra collapsing. Sam went over to her and assisted by Rina, was able to revive her.

Sandra was unable to get on her feet unassisted. An ambulance was called for, which took Sandra to the Emergency Room of nearby hospital. She was hospitalized.

Chapter Seventy Five

March 18, 1994 · Diary to Lauren Morgan

March 18, 1994   Diary to Lauren Morgan

Worry and depression.

My attitude at office seems to be sullen in silence, as it was at times with Lauren. Have thoughts of drinking to relieve my worries. Keep judging pros and cons of my drinking again—controlled. Maybe foolish but seems possible. But I need my wits about me in dealing with the detective and what LeMay is trying to do. Detective spoke to me about Lauren still missing, in which he asked, "From Riker's Island you went to live at a rooming house?"

"Yes."

"From where you continued to visit Lauren Morgan?"

"Yes, I was hoping that after some time and distance between us and I got to working, she would come to think lovingly of me again. I loved her so much. I can't help thinking of her as part of me. Her missing now is part of me missing."

He asked me how many times I violated the court restraining order not to go near Lauren.

I said I hadn't counted the number of times. He wormed out of me that it had been a good number of times and added that it could mean felony charges against me. He then asked me what my general reaction was when Lauren Morgan took up with LeMay.

"I was not happy about it," I said.

"You were jealous? Enough for some kind of revenge?"

"Not that I'd do anything to cause her to be missing."

Following this, I went to my room where Beth told me the detective questioned her about Lauren. She said I told the detective, "Lauren told me that when she had seen LeMay taking opium he had said stomach pains had driven him to take it for relief. Lauren said LeMay had tried to influence her to take opium and she had said she had enough of a problem with drinking. It seemed to make her outgoing personality more outgoing, which LeMay had not ceased to notice, upon hearing her talking about him in connection with drugs and questionable characters, causing LeMay to remind her if she couldn't keep to herself certain things about him, she could be silenced. Lauren said LeMay mentioned it to her in a manner that made her blood run cold. She, nevertheless, continued her relationship with LeMay, thinking she could control her relationship with him."

Shut myself in my room and listened to violin piece—Dvorak Romance Opus 11—pretty melody. Watched TV garbage in which, to distance myself from it, I escaped into sleep.

March 20, 1994   Diary to Lauren Morgan

Hate, like a cancer, builds up and eats away. Listened to Swan Lake excerpts—Greig's Heartlands and The Late Spring; beautiful. Went to Columbia-Presbyterian Hospital to see son. No heart donor available for him.

Chapter Seventy Six

March 21, 1994   Diary to Lauren Morgan

Confined, with no social life getting to me. Left knee has arthritis ache. Contacted by detective who said LeMay told him Lauren had mentioned to him that I put handfulls of Ajax cleaner powder in her best plant. I said I felt so full of remorse and guilt, I had to admit to Lauren what I had done and helped her to clean it out.

"You don't think Lauren Morgan might have got to thinking you might put Ajax cleanser powder into her food?" the detective said.

"In any case, I didn't."

The detective added, "LeMay says Lauren Morgan told him you threatened her with, "You're going to the hospital."

"Meaning I would go with her, as she had gone with me, to the hospital for an ailing condition." I also asked if LeMay had an attorney.

"One of the most expensive," the detective answered.

"LeMay has also said that Lauren Morgan told him you kept a diary."

Chapter Seventy Seven

March 27, 1994   Diary to Lauren Morgan

Tired with fear and depression over the weekend. See need for attorney. Will contact Legal Aid. More dream, unsettling.

Went to see my son at Columbia-Presbyterian Hospital. I could see the boy was well aware if he didn't get another heart, he would die. A pediatric cardiologist came in while I was with the boy. He checked the boy's condition, took me aside and said, "His need for a heart is no less desperate than it was yesterday. One of the unpleasant things about the job—lack of hearts available for transplant. We have one patient, a boy, whose heart has been struck down by what could be a virus that laid waste to his organs. He has been in intensive care for five weeks and will die if he doesn't get a heart in time. We lose about a quarter of the children on heart transplant lists because there aren't enough hearts available for transplant— enough donated hearts. This boy's condition has gone from bad to worse since he fell ill with what appeared to be the flu. Not HIV virus. Cardiomyopathy—damage to a heart caused by a virus. He's now on artificial support. It's something you don't think will happen in your wildest nightmares. His chances grow slimmer with each day that passes. If he had received a heart earlier when he was stronger, he would have had a 90% chance of a good outcome. In his struggle his heart would have stopped if he hadn't been put on heart support. He had had seizures and now he has a 50-50 chance—postponement causing other of his body systems to fall apart. He had a strong will to live. We do the best we can to keep them going so that if a heart comes along, they'll be in the best possible shape to receive it. The public doesn't have enough guidance in the need for heart donation—not enough. It needs an all-out advertising and public relations media blitz to make those outside aware— like what we get when a new blockbuster movie is launched or when a high-powered politician campaigns for re-election."

Chapter Seventy Eight

March 28, 1994   Diary to Lauren Morgan

Went to Legal Aid. Helen Cleary, quiet, worn, thin, serious woman in her late forties was assigned to me. I told her about my marriage, the baby girl we had adopted that passed away, my ailing son in need of a heart donor, my separation from my wife, my meeting Lauren and our living together, my drinking problem and loss of job, the big argument between me and Lauren, her court order barring me from going near her, our second big argument, my continuing to see Lauren while the court restraining order was in effect, Lauren meeting LeMay, Lauren's disappearance, my questioning by police and detective and my need for her especially after being asked for my diary by an ADA. Helen Cleary borrowed my diary.

March 29, 1994   Diary to Lauren Morgan

Feel lousy and lazy. Legs weak. Saw my attorney, Mrs. Cleary, who returned my diary after having made a copy for herself. She said while pointing in the diary, "The entry about setting out with a .38 caliber hand gun with silencer to kill Lauren Morgan and LeMay…"

"I'm afraid of that too," I said. "And no success yet in finding out what happened to Lauren."

"She would have had no motive for committing suicide?"

"No, no, no."

"We have inferences on the part of two suspects being played against each other."

"And with the diary?"

"More than inferences."

"Strong enough for them to prosecute?"

"They could be waiting for more to do with."

"How long?" I asked.

"Difficult to say. Let me see what I can come up with."

March 30, 1994   Diary to Lauren Morgan

My attorney called me at the office. Reviewing my diary again. I asked if there's any way I could refuse to hand my diary over to ADA. She didn't think so. Asked attorney if they could jail me after looking through my diary.

"Depends on how much corroboration they can come up with," she said.

March 31, 1994   Diary to Lauren Morgan

Went to see my son in Columbia-Presbyterian Hospital. No heart donor available for him. He needs one now or he'll die. I hugged him, feeling this could be the last time I'd see him. Said good-bye.

With Lauren still missing, LeMay always trying to downgrade me as if I'm responsible for her missing. Only suspects are me and LeMay. I know it's not me. Waiting, something my son and I don't have any more time for.

Wrote a suicide note stressing my heart be made available to my son. Feeling strongly that LeMay is responsible for Lauren's disappearance I got out my .38 hand gun with silencer to seek out LeMay and do away with him before taking care of myself. My suicide note will be found on me directing a heart transplant team do what it has been trained to do, so my son, after undergoing the heart transplant operation, will have my heart ticking in his chest.

Felt a tremendous urge for drinking, as a sort of last meal before the end and as a fillip to get going on what I have to do. Bought a bottle of scotch.

Now 4:30 p.m., alone in my small room. Test begins with Dewars scotch. None of boss's business what I do with my personal life. Whether he does or doesn't put me on the payroll won't matter anyway. Has been grand illusion and/or grand self-deception. Seeing I have the will and character to drink sensibly and get on with my task.

5:00 p.m.—A small buzz and feeling of well-being. Stimulation in mind and body and thought (ideas). Can't have any loss of memory. Aware in using this as a last drink nerve builder, I'm walking a fine line. If I re-read my diary with this stimulation, could I see things in it that could be helpful? In writing my diary, I should have asked myself first if I would be writing anything which a prosecutor could use against me. Doesn't matter now anyway. Clearly, my son has much more to live for than I. Though my time is running out, I will live on in him. Must be completely Jekyll about this. Any changes in behavior (animation, cheerfulness, confidence) would be completely out of character with former coolness, sullenness, detachment, silence.

Alcohol hitting my blood stream and buzz is beautiful. Alone in my too small room listening to Sibelius' Symphony

#2, dreaming the impossible dream of retiring in Alabama on Lake Tate with savings for down payment on a house.

Now time for spray. Wonder if there's problem with drink and spray mixing. Possible problem if I drink alone here, I'll be just sober enough for scheduled events. Drink has already quite stimulated me. I think, at least without an excuse, that this outlet is necessary, like a man's last meal before going to the gallows. Aware of a tremendous feeling of well-being, energy and thoughts. Nothing now could make me feel less than fully confident and in control.

Thinking about my downfall as a possible best seller to make me carefree money-wise for life (what life?). Its chances as best seller greatly enhanced if I die through some unnatural cause or by my own hand. Isn't taking an over-doze of pills literally dying by your own hand? Actually not a bad, if not beautiful way to go; especially if done at the height of fantasy in drinking. Done when dead tired and we pass on in our sleep. Beats shooting, knifing, hanging, jumping off a building or bridge or rotting away taking one day at a time.

Maugham's stories (always readable) become delectable because of savory words usually passed by to get to the meaning of the phrase faster. Eyesight now absolutely keen. Grandiose ideas now about getting story of my downfall typed (using 2 typists so they don't get the whole idea). What a boon to mankind I've become after only an hour or so of testing. Now the ideas come, each one better than the one before… Should I call Alan Amchile to ask his opinion then, without waiting for his answer, my own answer? I now have a tic in my right eye. When errors appear in text, sometimes better not to correct through editing, but even then, the editing through demo Hyde can require editing, and then who is editing who?

Drinking now getting quite well acquainted with me. Knocked over water bottle. It's really time to stop for test purposes. Demon Hyde may acquire a grasp on me. Cannot lose sight of what's before me for the sake of my son and me. Don't want to get signs my system not used to former appetite for alcohol. Take hold there. Come on, character and will and Jekyll, show your stuff against demon Hyde.

Now all encircled with well-being. Don't want to get to thinking that to not interrupt this would be an insult to my will and character. Having a reason to beware of the possible start of a breakdown. A hint was that, I knocked over my water that spilled on the rug and excused it to myself by saying it was part of the rug I didn't vacuum that has now been made cleaner. I was also intending to reach for asthma spray but grabbed scotch instead—demon Hyde, trying to play a trick on me, which was repulsed, thanks to Jekyll, who has me feeling unless I stop this test shortly—I meant to say "now" instead of "shortly". Score against demon Hyde. Control? Has not been kissed good-bye. It's not gone, thanks to me and character and Jekyll against demon Hyde. I know I can win this because it's a matter of life and death. It's raining out. I have no place to go, no one to impress, nothing else to do immediately. Is the weather conspiring to keep me here? I can stop this now. No, I have to stop this, now. Sorry, demon Hyde, I have prevented you from being able to gloat at me with glee. You haven't beaten me. Don't try to tell me you'll get me next time after that, because I won't be around, which may give you something to gloat over, not with callousness nor malignance, I allow you—I really can't hate you. You're not outside. You're within.

Could possibly have prolonged this test, but because of long layoff from drink, I couldn't risk it. If you are cursed with alcoholism, you live in apprehension and anxiety of what you are capable of and might do or you live in loneliness, horror and fear of what you can't attempt. Is something like a faint mind transference trying to get through to me? It could only come from one person, if I am not imagining…Is she alive or contacting me from beyond the grave? Where is she? Where is Lauren? She doesn't know. Her head has been hurt. What has happened? She has been kidnapped…By whom? She doesn't know. Was LeMay connected with it? She doesn't know. The kidnappers want ransom money. From whom? LeMay.

Chapter Seventy Nine

The following day, Mark, with a slight hangover, his face puffy, pathetic and pale like a clown's, communicated to the police his having been contacted by mental telepathy from Lauren and what had passed between them. The police seemed skeptical, until they heard from LeMay that he had received a communication from kidnappers that they had Lauren and wanted $1,000,000 from him for her release.

LeMay informed the police he would pay the $1,000,000 for Lauren's release. The release was made with $1,000,000.

When LeMay met with Lauren he said, after her thanking him, he had not realized how much he needed her until he had the feeling she might be gone for good. He added, "My wife and I are getting divorced."

Lauren told him her husband wouldn't give her a divorce unless he had her apartment, which she wanted for herself.

"If he'll take its value in money instead, perhaps I can be of assistance," LeMay suggested.

She thanked him.

Lauren met with Mark, who passed on to her that as no heart had been forthcoming for his son, he would forfeit his own for his son. Lauren made it known she would do what she could to get a heart for Mark's son.

Lauren went after LeMay's help in getting a heart for Mark's son. LeMay told her for a huge cash sum, he could get a heart for Mark's son, which he would pay for if she would marry him when they are free to. Lauren's reaction was if LeMay would get a heart donor for Mark's son, she would marry him.

A heart was obtained for Mark's son. The heart transplant took place. Mark's son survived.

Chapter Eighty

Mark, having heard his wife, Sandra, had been hospitalized, where she was diagnosed as having undergone a stroke, went to see her in the hospital. She said it was nice of him to come and see her and explained that she had been exercising in a gym, after jogging, when she felt herself weaken and collapsed.

"What kind of exercise?" Mark asked.

"Shadow boxing."

"Had you been boxing?"

"Not that day. Previously, I had trained and been in a novice boxing match in the Golden Gloves. It was a fight I won and I was going to go a step further to have another fight."

"Could have got to be too much for you."

"One of the thirteen women who trained where I was, used to say, 'Instead of getting angry at your husband, go down to the gym and box a few rounds."

"Do me a favor in the future?"

"Of course."

"Get angry with me instead."

"Of course," Sandra said. "It's a vicious sport—takes a lot of dedication—not easy."

"I don't disagree," Mark said.

"Girls want to do the most they can do and boys get confused by it."

"I've been confused."

"I'll make it up to you. Men feel women have invaded their male world and get their egos hurt."

"What did they do down at your gym when there weren't enough sparring partners to box with the experienced competitive female boxers?"

"Like Rina. You should have seen her. I was immediately taken by her warm and friendly manner, giving no indication of the power she had in unleashing awesome upper-cut and round-house blows to the head and body. She boxed with men as part of her training. Women always wanted to compete but the authorities had this thing about women boxers. But it has caught on and there are no signs of it going downhill. It was a great experience."

"I hope you've had enough."

"I have," Sandra said.

"I'm glad to hear that."

"I'm pleased it pleases you."

"I think you're going to be OK."

"I hope so, for your sake," Sandra said.

In the hospital corridor, Mark met Sandra's doctor.

"She's changing," Mark said. "I wouldn't go so far as to say a stroke can be a good thing, but it's changing my wife back toward her old sweet loving self."

"A stroke can definitely alter behavior," the doctor said.

Mark, most thankful to Lauren for being responsible for obtaining a heart donor for his son, revealed his wife's change, together with his wish for a small apartment for him, his wife and son. There had been talk at the firm Mark was doing work for of him being put on the payroll, which had not yet taken place. Lauren felt it would need some extra push for it to happen.

Lauren spoke to LeMay about letting Mark handle some of his portfolio of stocks and bonds that she was handling so Mark could use it as a bargaining incentive with the firm in which he was hoping to be place on payroll. Holding Lauren responsible for monitoring what Mark would be doing, LeMay was willing to go along with Lauren's suggestions.

Mark kept to himself about his having broken off one night his non-drinking record. The only reason he did it he thought was that everything had got to be too much for him, including what he thought at the time would be the going through of his suicide.

Mark took his suggestion package to his firm who, seeing added business, it would bring them, put him on their payroll. With this done, Mark was able to rent a small apartment for him and his wife along with the blessing of having their son with a new heart with them.

Though the strong bond between Mark and Lauren ceased to be physical, their thought transference communication between each other did not cease.

Could the bond between Mark and Lauren have been on a plane beyond love?